Colonial Architecture
of Cape Cod, Nantucket
and Martha's Vineyard

Doorway of the Oldest House on Nantucket   Date 1686

NANTUCKET, JETHRO COFFIN HOUSE

Colonial Architecture of Cape Cod, Nantucket and Martha's Vineyard

ALFRED EASTON POOR

DOVER PUBLICATIONS, INC., NEW YORK

Copyright © 1932 by William Helburn, Inc.

Published in Canada by General Publishing Company, Ltd., 30 Lesmill Road, Don Mills, Toronto, Ontario.
Published in the United Kingdom by Constable and Company, Ltd., 10 Orange Street, London WC 2.

This Dover edition, first published in 1970, is an unabridged and unaltered republication of the work originally published by William Helburn, Inc., New York, in 1932.

Standard Book Number: 486-22375-2
Library of Congress Catalog Card Number: 78-108778

Manufactured in the United States of America
Dover Publications, Inc.
180 Varick Street
New York, N.Y. 10014

FOREWORD

IN the preparation of this book, my purpose has been two-fold. First, to make a record of the houses of our ancestors before time and "modernization" take too great a toll from existing examples. Second, to show the beauty that these houses achieve through simplicity and straightforward plan, in the hope that it may be an inspiration to those who are now building our smaller houses, and to those who feel the unique value of the "Cape Cod House" as a distinctively American contribution to Architecture.

Cape Cod, Nantucket and Martha's Vineyard have been grouped together because the architecture of all three, while very similar and with a common flavor of the sea, differs markedly from that of the rest of New England. The influence of those who followed the sea in sailing ships, or who helped to build them, is seen in the sturdy type of construction, in the common use of panelling on the interior, in the compactness of the plan, and particularly in the bowed roof which, one is told by their descendants, the shipwrights built to resemble the bottom of a ship. It is interesting, also, to note the variation of the architecture in different localities and to follow the hand of a certain carpenter-builder by the prevalence in a neighborhood of a characteristic fanlight, a distinctive cornice, or a curiously-shaped pilaster.

Though the whole district abounds in history and tradition, harking back to November 21st, 1620, when the Mayflower anchored in Provincetown harbor, architectural merit rather than mere historical interest has been the deciding factor in the choice of material.

Having found in my own architectural work that no material on Cape Cod had been collected in book form, I was prompted to take these photographs and make these measured drawings during the course of many visits to Cape Cod, and to the two islands, Nantucket and Martha's Vineyard.

Thus many houses are now published for the first time, and material made available which will, I hope, be of as much value and interest to others as the collecting of it has been for me.

Without the invaluable and enthusiastic help of the following people many of the finest of the houses could never have been photographed: the late Mr. Herbert Ten Broeck Jacquelin, Mrs. Margaret H. Richardson, and Mr. Raymond Moore, all of Cape Cod; Mr. William F. Macy, president of the Nantucket Historical Association; and Mrs. Price Post of Martha's Vineyard and New York. I am glad of this opportunity to acknowledge gratefully their many courtesies.

ALFRED EASTON POOR

New York City, August, 1932

"To My Wife
For Her Encouragement and Help".

LIST OF PLATES

FRONTISPIECE. Nantucket, Jethro Coffin House, Doorway.

ONE STOREY HOUSES

PLATE 1. Nantucket, Jethro Coffin House.
PLATE 2. Cape Cod, Dennis, Jorgenson House.
PLATE 3. Cape Cod, Old House near Sandwich.
PLATE 4. Cape Cod, Brewster, "Sunnyside" (*upper*).
Cape Cod, Bass River, "Bass River Farm" (*lower*).
PLATE 5. Cape Cod, Barnstable, "Jacquelin Cottage" (*upper*).
Cape Cod, Half House, near Sandwich (*lower*).
PLATE 6. Cape Cod, Barnstable, "Amos Otis House". Two Views.
PLATE 7. Cape Cod, An Old House. Two Views.
PLATE 8. Cape Cod, Barnstable (*upper*).
Cape Cod, near Brewster (*lower*).
PLATE 9. Cape Cod, South Yarmouth. Typical Houses.
PLATE 10. Cape Cod, Quivet Neck (*upper*).
Cape Cod, Provincetown (*lower*).
PLATE 11. Cape Cod, Dennis, "Richardson Cottage".
PLATE 12. Cape Cod, Dennis, "Half" House (*upper*).
Cape Cod, House near Brewster (*lower*).
PLATE 13. Martha's Vineyard, West Tisbury.
PLATE 14. Cape Cod, near Truro.
PLATE 15. Cape Cod, Barnstable, "Jacqueline Guest House" (*upper*).
Cape Cod, Bass River (*lower*).
PLATE 16. Cape Cod, Dennis, "Judge Freaman House". Two Views.
PLATE 17. Cape Cod, Santuit, "Old Tavern".
PLATE 18. Cape Cod, Bass River, "Bass River Farm".

NOTE: Plates 4, 5, 18 and 19 illustrate examples of Bowed Roofed Houses.

TWO STOREY HOUSES

PLATE 19. Cape Cod, near Sandwich (*upper*).
Nantucket, Main Street (*lower*).
PLATE 20. Cape Cod, near Sandwich (*upper*).
Cape Cod, near Barnstable (*lower*).
PLATE 21. Plymouth, "Howland House".
PLATE 22. Nantucket. Example of a Double House (*upper*).
Martha's Vineyard, Edgartown, "Mayhew House" (*lower*).
PLATE 23. Cape Cod, Sandwich.
PLATE 24. Nantucket, Illustrations of Two Houses.

LIST OF PLATES

PLATE 25. Cape Cod, Falmouth (*upper*).
Cape Cod, South Yarmouth (*lower*).
PLATE 26. Nantucket, Illustrations of Two Houses.
PLATE 27. East Taunton.
PLATE 28. Nantucket, Center Street (*upper*).
Cape Cod, Falmouth (*lower*).
PLATE 29. Cape Cod, Barnstable (*upper*).
Nantucket, Main Street (*lower*).
PLATE 30. Martha's Vineyard, Edgartown.
PLATE 31. Cape Cod, Provincetown (*upper*).
Nantucket, Union Street (*lower*).
PLATE 32. Cape Cod, Dennis (*upper*).
Cape Cod, Falmouth (*lower*).
PLATE 33. Cape Cod, South Yarmouth.
PLATE 34. Nantucket, Center Street (*upper*).
Martha's Vineyard, Edgartown (*lower*).
PLATE 35. Martha's Vineyard, Edgartown.
PLATE 36. Martha's Vineyard, Edgartown (*upper*).
Nantucket, Union Street (*lower*).
PLATE 37. Cape Cod, Falmouth (*upper*).
Nantucket, "Macy House" (*lower*).
PLATE 38. Cape Cod, Provincetown. Illustrations of Two Houses.
PLATE 39. Cape Cod, Barnstable, "The Blue Blinds".
PLATE 40. Plymouth, "Antiquarian Society" (*upper*).
Cape Cod, Falmouth (*lower*).
PLATE 41. Cape Cod, Falmouth.
PLATE 42. Nantucket, "Moor's End". Two Views.
PLATE 43. Nantucket, Main Street. Illustrations of Two Houses.
PLATE 44. Cape Cod, South Yarmouth.
PLATE 45. Plymouth (*upper*).
Nantucket, Orange Street (*lower*).
PLATE 46. Plymouth.
PLATE 47. Cape Cod, Barnstable (*upper*).
Cape Cod, An Old House (*lower*).
PLATE 48. Martha's Vineyard, Edgartown. Illustrations of Two Houses.
PLATE 49. Cape Cod, Provincetown, Commercial Street (*upper*).
Nantucket, Main Street (*lower*).
PLATE 50. Plymouth, "Shaw House" (*upper*).
Cape Cod, Barnstable (*lower*).
PLATE 51. Nantucket, Orange Street.

THREE STOREY HOUSES, WINDMILLS, BARNS, OUT BUILDINGS, FENCES AND CORNICES

PLATE 52. Nantucket, Center Street (*upper*).
Martha's Vineyard, Edgartown (*lower*).

LIST OF PLATES

PLATE 53. Plymouth (*upper*).
    Nantucket, "Pacific Club" (*lower*).
PLATE 54. Nantucket, Windmill (*left*).
    Cape Cod, near Truro, Windmill (*right*).
PLATE 55. Cape Cod, Illustrations of Two Barns.
PLATE 56. Plymouth, Barn of "Antiquarian Society" (*upper*).
    Cape Cod, Santuit, Woodshed of "Old Tavern" (*lower*).
PLATE 57. Nantucket, Stable of "Moor's End".
PLATE 58. Nantucket, Stable of "Moor's End" (*left*).
    Cape Cod, Stable near Barnstable (*right*).
PLATE 59. Martha's Vineyard, Edgartown. Typical Fence (*upper*).
    Martha's Vineyard, Edgartown. Typical Fence (*center*).
    Nantucket, Fair Street. Typical Fence (*lower*).
PLATE 60. East Taunton, Cornice (*left*).
    Nantucket, Union Street. Cornice and Quoins (*right*).
PLATE 61. Martha's Vineyard, Edgartown. Illustrations of Two Cornices.
PLATE 62. Cape Cod, Barnstable, Cornice (*upper*).
    Cape Cod, Provincetown, Cornice (*lower*).
PLATE 63. Nantucket, North Street.

WINDOWS

PLATE 64. Nantucket, "Jethro Coffin House".
PLATE 65. Cape Cod, Sandwich, "The Lindens" (*left*).
    Cape Cod, Barnstable (*right*).
PLATE 66. Martha's Vineyard, Edgartown (*left*).
    Nantucket, Center Street (*right*).
PLATE 67. Cape Cod, Provincetown (*left*).
    Martha's Vineyard, Edgartown (*right*).
PLATE 68. Cape Cod, West Barnstable (*left*).
    Cape Cod, Provincetown (*right*).
PLATE 69. Cape Cod, South Yarmouth. Window and Iron Balcony.
PLATE 70. Cape Cod, Quivet Neck. Characteristic Doorway and Windows.

DOORWAYS AND PORTICOS

PLATE 71. Nantucket, Pleasant Street.
PLATE 72. Cape Cod, Provincetown (*left*).
    Nantucket, "Unitarian Church" (*right*).
PLATE 73. Cape Cod, Dennis. Illustrations of Two Doorways.
PLATE 74. Cape Cod, Bass River. Two Views.
PLATE 75. Plymouth (*left*).
    Cape Cod, Provincetown (*right*).
PLATE 76. Cape Cod, Barnstable (*left*).
    Cape Cod, Sandwich (*right*).
PLATE 77. Martha's Vineyard, Edgartown. Illustrations of Two Doorways.
PLATE 78. Cape Cod, Provincetown. Illustrations of Two Doorways.

LIST OF PLATES

PLATE 79. Cape Cod, near Sandwich (*left*).
Cape Cod, Santuit (*right*).
PLATE 80. East Taunton (*left*).
Plymouth (*right*).
PLATE 81. Nantucket, Orange Street (*left*).
Nantucket, Center Street (*right*).
PLATE 82. Martha's Vineyard, Edgartown (*left*).
Cape Cod, South Yarmouth (*right*).
PLATE 83. Martha's Vineyard, Edgartown (*left*).
Cape Cod, Santuit (*right*).
PLATE 84. Nantucket, "Methodist Church" (*left*).
Cape Cod, near Truro (*right*).
PLATE 85. Martha's Vineyard, Edgartown. Illustrations of Two Doorways.
PLATE 86. Nantucket, Orange Street (*left*).
Cape Cod, Provincetown (*right*).
PLATE 87. Nantucket (*left*)
Nantucket, Pleasant Street (*right*).
PLATE 88. Cape Cod, Provincetown (*left*).
Nantucket, Main Street (*right*).
PLATE 89. Martha's Vineyard, Edgartown. Illustrations of Two Doorways.
PLATE 90. Nantucket, Federal Street (*left*).
Nantucket, Fair Street (*right*).
PLATE 91. Nantucket, Center Street.
PLATE 92. Nantucket, "Macy House".
PLATE 93. Nantucket, Union Street.
PLATE 94. Nantucket, Orange Street.
PLATE 95. Martha's Vineyard, Edgartown.
PLATE 96. Cape Cod, Provincetown.
PLATE 97. Martha's Vineyard, Edgartown.
PLATE 98. Cape Cod, Provincetown, Commercial Street.
PLATE 99. Plymouth (*left*).
Martha's Vineyard, Edgartown (*right*).
PLATE 100. Cape Cod, Sandwich (*upper*).
Cape Cod, Falmouth (*lower*).
PLATE 101. Cape Cod, Falmouth. Illustrations of Two Porticos.

INTERIORS

PLATE 102. Nantucket, "Jethro Coffin House". Illustrations of Two Fireplaces.
PLATE 103. Cape Cod, Barnstable, "Jacquelin Cottage".
PLATE 104. Nantucket, North Street.
PLATE 105. Cape Cod, Sandwich, "The Lindens".
PLATE 106. Cape Cod, Barnstable, "Jacquelin Guest House" (*upper*).
Cape Cod, Barnstable, "Jacquelin Cottage" (*lower*).
PLATE 107. Cape Cod, Dennis, "Jorgenson House".

LIST OF PLATES

PLATE 108. Cape Cod, Barnstable, "The Blue Blinds" (*upper*).
Nantucket, "India House" (*lower*).
PLATE 109. Cape Cod, Dennis, "Motor Car Inn".
PLATE 110. Nantucket, "India House" (*upper*).
Cape Cod, Dennis, "Motor Car Inn" (*lower*).
PLATE 111. Cape Cod, Sandwich, "The Lindens" (*upper*).
Cape Cod, New Boston, near Dennis, "Judah Howes House" (*lower*).
PLATE 112. Cape Cod, Dennis, "Motor Car Inn" (*upper*).
Cape Cod, Dennis, "Richardson Cottage" (*lower*).
PLATE 113. Cape Cod, New Boston, near Dennis, "Judah Howes House" (*left*).
Cape Cod, Dennis, "Judge Freaman House" (*right*).
PLATE 114. Cape Cod, Dennis, "Motor Car Inn" (*upper*).
Cape Cod, Dennis, "Judge Freaman House" (*lower*).
PLATE 115. Cape Cod, Dennis, "Judge Freaman House". Old Kitchen (*upper*).
Cape Cod, Dennis, "Judge Freaman House". Parlor Windows (*lower*).
PLATE 116. Nantucket, "India House".
PLATE 117. Cape Cod, Dennis, "Judge Freaman House".

MEASURED DRAWINGS

PLATE 118. Cape Cod, Three Typical Houses.
PLATE 119. Cape Cod, Dennis, "Motor Car Inn", Front Entrance.
PLATE 120. Cape Cod, Dennis, "Judge Freaman House", Front Door.
PLATE 121. Cape Cod, Provincetown, Typical Doorway.
PLATE 122. Cape Cod, Bass River. Entrance Doorway.
PLATE 123. East Taunton. Entrance Doorway.
PLATE 124. Cape Cod, Dennis, "Judge Freaman House". Old Kitchen.
PLATE 125. Cape Cod, Dennis, "Judge Freaman House. Old Kitchen.
PLATE 126. Cape Cod, Dennis, "Judge Freaman House". Parlor.
PLATE 127. Cape Cod, Dennis, "Judge Freaman House". Parlor.
PLATE 128. Cape Cod, Dennis, "Jorgenson House". Parlor.
PLATE 129. Cape Cod, Dennis, "Jorgenson House". Parlor.
PLATE 130. Nantucket, "Jethro Coffin House". Fireplaces.
PLATE 131. Cape Cod, Dennis, "Motor Car Inn". Kitchen Fireplace.
PLATE 132. Cape Cod, Dennis, "Motor Car Inn". Parlor Fireplace.
PLATE 133. New Boston, "Judah Howes House". Stairs.
PLATE 134. Cape Cod, Dennis, "Judge Freaman House". Stairway.
PLATE 135. Cape Cod. Typical Floor Patterns and Splatters.

PLATE 1

Oldest House on Nantucket

NANTUCKET, "JETHRO COFFIN HOUSE"

Date 1686

PLATE 2

Typical One Storey House CAPE COD, DENNIS, JORGENSON HOUSE, TYPICAL *Date About 1750*

CAPE COD, OLD HOUSE NEAR SANDWICH

PLATE 4

CAPE COD, BREWSTER, "SUNNYSIDE"

Side View, Front View Illustrated on Plate 18

CAPE COD, BASS RIVER, "BASS RIVER FARM"
(Example of a Bowed Roof)

PLATE 5

Interiors illustrated on Plates 103 and 106
CAPE COD, BARNSTABLE, "JACQUELIN COTTAGE"

Example of Bowed Roof
CAPE COD, "HALF" HOUSE NEAR SANDWICH

PLATE 6

Rear View *Date 1745*

Front View *Date 1745*

CAPE COD, BARNSTABLE, AMOS OTIS HOUSE

PLATE 7

Rear View

Front View

CAPE COD, OLD HOUSE

Plate 8

CAPE COD, BARNSTABLE

CAPE COD, NEAR BREWSTER

PLATE 9

Typical Houses

CAPE COD, SOUTH YARMOUTH, KINGS HIGHWAY

PLATE 10

Doorway illustrated on Plate 70
CAPE COD, QUIVET NECK

CAPE COD, PROVINCETOWN

PLATE 11

Interior illustrated on Plate 112 CAPE COD, DENNIS, "RICHARDSON COTTAGE" *Date about 1780*

Typical "Half" House
CAPE COD, DENNIS

CAPE COD, KING'S HIGHWAY NEAR BREWSTER

MARTHA'S VINEYARD, WEST TISBURY

PLATE 14

CAPE COD, NEAR TRURO

PLATE 15

Interior illustrated on Plate 106
CAPE COD, BARNSTABLE, "JACQUELIN GUEST HOUSE"

Measured Drawing of Doorway, Plate 122. Doorway illustrated on Plate 74
CAPE COD, BASS RIVER

Plate 16

Side View   *Date, about 1732*

Front View   *Date, about 1732*
Additional illustrations, Plates 73, 113, 114, 115
Measured Drawing on Plate 120

CAPE COD, DENNIS, "JUDGE FREAMAN HOUSE"
(Typical "Salt Box" House)

PLATE 17

Doorway illustrated on Plate 79

CAPE COD, SANTUIT, OLD TAVERN

PLATE 18

Front View. Side View illustrated on Plate 4

CAPE COD, BASS RIVER, "BASS RIVER FARM"
(Example of a Bowed Roof)

PLATE 19

Doorway illustrated on Plate 79
CAPE COD, NEAR SANDWICH (Example of a Bowed Roof)

NANTUCKET, MAIN STREET

PLATE 20

"Salt Box" House
CAPE COD, NEAR SANDWICH

"Salt Box" House
CAPE COD, NEAR BARNSTABLE

PLATE 21

Date 1666

Doorway Illustrated on Plate 75

PLYMOUTH, "HOWLAND HOUSE"

PLATE 22

Double House
NANTUCKET

Doorway illustrated on Plate 89
MARTHA'S VINEYARD, EDGARTOWN, "MAYHEW HOUSE"

PLATE 23

Note Clustered Chimney   CAPE COD, SANDWICH   *Date 1640*

PLATE 24

NANTUCKET, WEST CENTER STREET

NANTUCKET, ORANGE STREET

PLATE 25

CAPE COD, FALMOUTH

CAPE COD, SOUTH YARMOUTH

PLATE 26

NANTUCKET, SUMMER STREET

Doorway illustrated on Plate 71
NANTUCKET, PLEASANT STREET

PLATE 27

Measured Drawing Plate 123. Additional illustrated details, Plates 60 and 80
EAST TAUNTON

PLATE 28

NANTUCKET, CENTER STREET

CAPE COD, FALMOUTH

PLATE 29

CAPE COD, BARNSTABLE

NANTUCKET, MAIN STREET

PLATE 30

MARTHA'S VINEYARD, EDGARTOWN

Doorway illustrated on Plate 95

PLATE 31

CAPE COD, PROVINCETOWN

NANTUCKET, UNION STREET

CAPE COD, DENNIS

Parapet illustrated on Plate 100

CAPE COD, FALMOUTH

PLATE 33

Doorway illustrated on Plate 82
CAPE COD, SOUTH YARMOUTH, TYPICAL TWO STOREY HOUSE

PLATE 34

Note "Captain's Walk"
NANTUCKET, CENTER STREET

MARTHA'S VINEYARD, EDGARTOWN

PLATE 35

MARTHA'S VINEYARD, EDGARTOWN

Doorway illustrated on Plate 97

PLATE 36

MARTHA'S VINEYARD, EDGARTOWN

Additional illustrated Details, Plates 60 and 93
NANTUCKET, 18 UNION STREET

PLATE 37

CAPE COD, FALMOUTH

Doorway illustrated on Plate 92
NANTUCKET, "MACY HOUSE"

PLATE 38

CAPE COD, PROVINCETOWN

Doorway illustrated on Plate 98
CAPE COD, PROVINCETOWN

PLATE 39

CAPE COD, BARNSTABLE, "THE BLUE BLINDS"

Interior illustrated on Plate 108

PLATE 40

PLYMOUTH, ANTIQUARIAN SOCIETY

CAPE COD, FALMOUTH

PLATE 41

CAPE COD, FALMOUTH

Portico illustrated on Plate 101

PLATE 42

Rear View

View from Garden

NANTUCKET, "MOOR'S END"

PLATE 43

NANTUCKET, MAIN STREET

NANTUCKET, MAIN STREET

PLATE 44

Window and Iron Balcony illustrated on Plate 69

CAPE COD, SOUTH YARMOUTH

PLATE 45

PLYMOUTH

NANTUCKET, ORANGE STREET

PLATE 46

PLYMOUTH

PLATE 47

CAPE COD, BARNSTABLE

Note "Captain's Walk"
CAPE COD, OLD HOUSE

PLATE 48

MARTHA'S VINEYARD, EDGARTOWN

MARTHA'S VINEYARD, EDGARTOWN

PLATE 49

CAPE COD, PROVINCETOWN, COMMERCIAL STREET

Doorway illustrated on Plate 88
NANTUCKET, MAIN STREET

PLATE 50

Date 1701

PLYMOUTH, "SHAW HOUSE"

Additional illustrated details on Plates 65 and 76

CAPE COD, BARNSTABLE

PLATE 51

Note "Captain's Walk"   NANTUCKET, ORANGE STREET

PLATE 52

Three Storey House. Note "Captain's Walk"
NANTUCKET, CENTER STREET

Three Storey House
MARTHA'S VINEYARD, EDGARTOWN

PLATE 53

Portico illustrated on Plate 99
PLYMOUTH

NANTUCKET, PACIFIC CLUB *Date 1772*

PLATE 54

Windmill   CAPE COD, KINGS HIGHWAY, NEAR TRURO

Windmill   *Date 1746*   NANTUCKET

PLATE 55

Barn
CAPE COD

Barn. Note Light over Door
CAPE COD

PLYMOUTH, BARN OF ANTIQUARIAN SOCIETY

CAPE COD, SANTUIT, WOODSHED OF OLD TAVERN

PLATE 57

NANTUCKET, STABLE OF "MOOR'S END"

PLATE 58

CAPE COD, STABLE NEAR BARNSTABLE

NANTUCKET, STABLE OF "MOOR'S END"

PLATE 59

MARTHA'S VINEYARD, EDGARTOWN

MARTHA'S VINEYARD, EDGARTOWN

NANTUCKET, FAIR STREET
Typical Fences

PLATE 60

Cornice and Quoins. House illustrated on Plate 36
NANTUCKET, 18 UNION STREET

Cornice. House illustrated on Plate 27
EAST TAUNTON

PLATE 61

Simple Cornice

Cornice with Brackets, Characteristic of Edgartown

MARTHA'S VINEYARD, EDGARTOWN

PLATE 62

Cornice showing Return and Corner Pilaster
CAPE COD, BARNSTABLE

Cornice showing typical Dentils
CAPE COD, PROVINCETOWN

PLATE 63

Note Corbelled cornice and clustered chimney. Interior illustrated on Plate 104
NANTUCKET, NORTH STREET

PLATE 64

Date 1686

Detail of Leaded Casements, Characteristic of Earlier Houses
NANTUCKET, JETHRO COFFIN HOUSE

PLATE 65

Typical 12 light window. House illustrated on Plate 50
CAPE COD, BARNSTABLE

Typical 24 light window.   Date about 1730
CAPE COD, SANDWICH, "THE LINDENS"

PLATE 66

Typical Projecting Frame and Cornice Mould
NANTUCKET, CENTER STREET

Note Wood Lintel
MARTHA'S VINEYARD, EDGARTOWN
Window of Historical Society

PLATE 67

Triple Hung Window
CAPE COD, PROVINCETOWN

Typical Wood Lintel and Rounded Frame
MARTHA'S VINEYARD, EDGARTOWN

PLATE 68

Detail of Window   Date 1847

CAPE COD, PROVINCETOWN,
CHURCH OF THE REDEEMER

Detail of Sliding Shutters

CAPE COD, WEST BARNSTABLE
FIRST CONGREGATIONAL CHURCH

PLATE 69

Window and Iron Balcony. House illustrated on Plate 44
CAPE COD, SOUTH YARMOUTH

PLATE 70

Characteristic Doorway and Windows. House illustrated on Plate 10
CAPE COD, QUIVET NECK

PLATE 71

Entrance Doorway. House illustrated on Plate 26
NANTUCKET, PLEASANT STREET

PLATE 72

Double Entrance Doorway *Date 1809*
NANTUCKET, UNITARIAN CHURCH

Doorway
CAPE COD, PROVINCETOWN, CHURCH OF THE REDEEMER

PLATE 73

Doorway Showing Typical Shutters.   Date about 1732
Measured Drawing on Plate 120
Additional Illustrations on Plates 16, 113, 114 and 115

CAPE COD, DENNIS, JUDGE FREAMAN HOUSE

Doorway showing Double Dentil Cornice. Date about 1780
Measured Drawing on Plate 119

CAPE COD, DENNIS, MOTOR CAR INN

PLATE 74

Entrance Doorway. Measured Drawing on Plate 122

House illustrated on Plate 15

CAPE COD, BASS RIVER

PLATE 75

Doorway   *Date 1666*
House illustrated on Plate 21
PLYMOUTH, "HOWLAND HOUSE"

Typical Doorway
CAPE COD, PROVINCETOWN

PLATE 76

Doorway   Date about 1730
CAPE COD, SANDWICH, "THE LINDENS"

Doorway. House illustrated on Plate 50
CAPE COD, BARNSTABLE

PLATE 77

Doorway MARTHA'S VINEYARD, EDGARTOWN

Doorway MARTHA'S VINEYARD, EDGARTOWN

PLATE 78

Doorway, Kazelaw House *Typical Doorway. Measured Drawing on Plate 121*

CAPE COD, PROVINCETOWN

PLATE 79

Doorway. House illustrated on Plate 17
CAPE COD, SANTUIT, OLD TAVERN

Doorway. House illustrated on Plate 19
CAPE COD, NEAR SANDWICH

PLATE 80

Doorway PLYMOUTH

Doorway. House illustrated on Plate 27
EAST TAUNTON

PLATE 81

Doorway NANTUCKET, CENTER STREET

Doorway NANTUCKET, 37 ORANGE STREET

PLATE 82

Doorway. House illustrated on Plate 33
CAPE COD, SOUTH YARMOUTH

Doorway
MARTHA'S VINEYARD, EDGARTOWN

PLATE 83

Doorway   CAPE COD, SANTUIT

Doorway   MARTHA'S VINEYARD, EDGARTOWN
CONGREGATIONAL CHURCH

PLATE 84

Doorway
CAPE COD, KING'S HIGHWAY, NEAR TRURO

Doorway
NANTUCKET, METHODIST CHURCH

PLATE 85

Doorway

Doorway

MARTHA'S VINEYARD EDGARTOWN

PLATE 86

Doorway   CAPE COD, PROVINCETOWN

Doorway and Steps   NANTUCKET, 38 ORANGE STREET

PLATE 87

Detail of House-front
NANTUCKET, PLEASANT STREET

Doorway
NANTUCKET

PLATE 88

Doorway CAPE COD, PROVINCETOWN

Doorway and Steps. House illustrated on Plate 49
NANTUCKET, MAIN STREET

PLATE 89

Typical Projecting Vestibule Doorway
MARTHA'S VINEYARD, EDGARTOWN

House illustrated on Plate 22
MARTHA'S VINEYARD, EDGARTOWN,
MAYHEW HOUSE

PLATE 90

Doorway and Steps
NANTUCKET, FAIR STREET

Doorway and Steps
NANTUCKET, FEDERAL STREET

PLATE 91

Doorway and Stoop

NANTUCKET, CENTER STREET

PLATE 92

Detail of Doorway. House illustrated on Plate 37
NANTUCKET, MACY HOUSE

PLATE 93

Entrance Doorway and Steps. House illustrated on Plate 36
NANTUCKET, 18 UNION STREET

PLATE 94

Double Doorway and Steps NANTUCKET, ORANGE STREET

PLATE 95

Doorway and Seats. House illustrated on Plate 30

MARTHA'S VINEYARD, EDGARTOWN

PLATE 96

CAPE COD, PROVINCETOWN

PLATE 97

Entrance Doorway. House illustrated on Plate 35
MARTHA'S VINEYARD, EDGARTOWN

PLATE 98

Vestibule and Doorway. House illustrated on Plate 38
CAPE COD, PROVINCETOWN, COMMERCIAL STREET

PLATE 99

Portico MARTHA'S VINEYARD, EDGARTOWN

Portico. House illustrated on Plate 53 PLYMOUTH

PLATE 100

Lattice Portico
CAPE COD, SANDWICH

House illustrated on Plate 32. Note Parapet
CAPE COD, FALMOUTH

PLATE 101

House illustrated on Plate 41

CAPE COD, FALMOUTH, PORTICOS

PLATE 102

Bedroom Fireplace. Measured Drawing on Plate 130

Parlor Fireplace. Measured Drawing on Plate 130
NANTUCKET, "JETHRO COFFIN HOUSE"

Interior. House illustrated on Plate 5. Interior illustrated on Plate 106
CAPE COD, BARNSTABLE, "JACQUELIN COTTAGE"

PLATE 104

Fireplace. House illustrated on Plate 63 NANTUCKET, NORTH STREET

PLATE 105

CAPE COD, SANDWICH, "THE LINDENS"

Fireplace

Fireplace. House illustrated on Plate 15
CAPE COD, BARNSTABLE, "JACQUELIN GUEST HOUSE"

Fireplace. House illustrated on Plate 5. Interior illustrated on Plate 103
CAPE COD, BARNSTABLE, "JACQUELIN COTTAGE"

PLATE 107

Parlor Fireplace. Measured Drawing on Plate 128
CAPE COD, DENNIS, "JORGENSON HOUSE"

PLATE 108

Parlor Fireplace. House illustrated on Plate 39
CAPE COD, BARNSTABLE, "THE BLUE BLINDS"

Parlor Fireplace
NANTUCKET, "INDIA HOUSE"

PLATE 109

Kitchen Fireplace. Measured Drawing on Plate 131
CAPE COD, DENNIS, "MOTOR CAR INN"

PLATE 110

Dining Room Fireplace
NANTUCKET, "INDIA HOUSE"

Parlor Fireplace. Measured Drawing on Plate 132
CAPE COD, DENNIS, "MOTOR CAR INN"

PLATE 111

Parlor Fireplace
CAPE COD, SANDWICH, "THE LINDENS"

Parlor Fireplace
CAPE COD, NEW BOSTON, NEAR DENNIS,
"JUDAH HOWES HOUSE"

PLATE 112

Fireplace and Panelling
CAPE COD, DENNIS, "MOTOR CAR INN"

Fireplace and Panelling. House illustrated on Plate 11
CAPE COD, DENNIS, "RICHARDSON COTTAGE"

PLATE 113

Stairs. Measured Drawing on Plate 134
CAPE COD, DENNIS,
"JUDGE FREAMAN HOUSE"

Stairs. Measured Drawing on Plate 133
CAPE COD, NEW BOSTON, NEAR DENNIS,
"JUDAH HOWES HOUSE"

Detail Wall with Sliding Shutter
CAPE COD, DENNIS, "MOTOR CAR INN"

Detail, Old Kitchen
CAPE COD, DENNIS, "JUDGE FREAMAN HOUSE"

PLATE 115

Old Kitchen. Measured Drawing on Plate 125

Parlor Windows. Measured Drawing on Plate 127

CAPE COD, DENNIS, "JUDGE FREAMAN HOUSE"

PLATE 116

Corner Cupboard

NANTUCKET, "INDIA HOUSE"

PLATE 117

Parlor. Measured Drawing on Plate 126

CAPE COD, DENNIS, "JUDGE FREAMAN HOUSE"

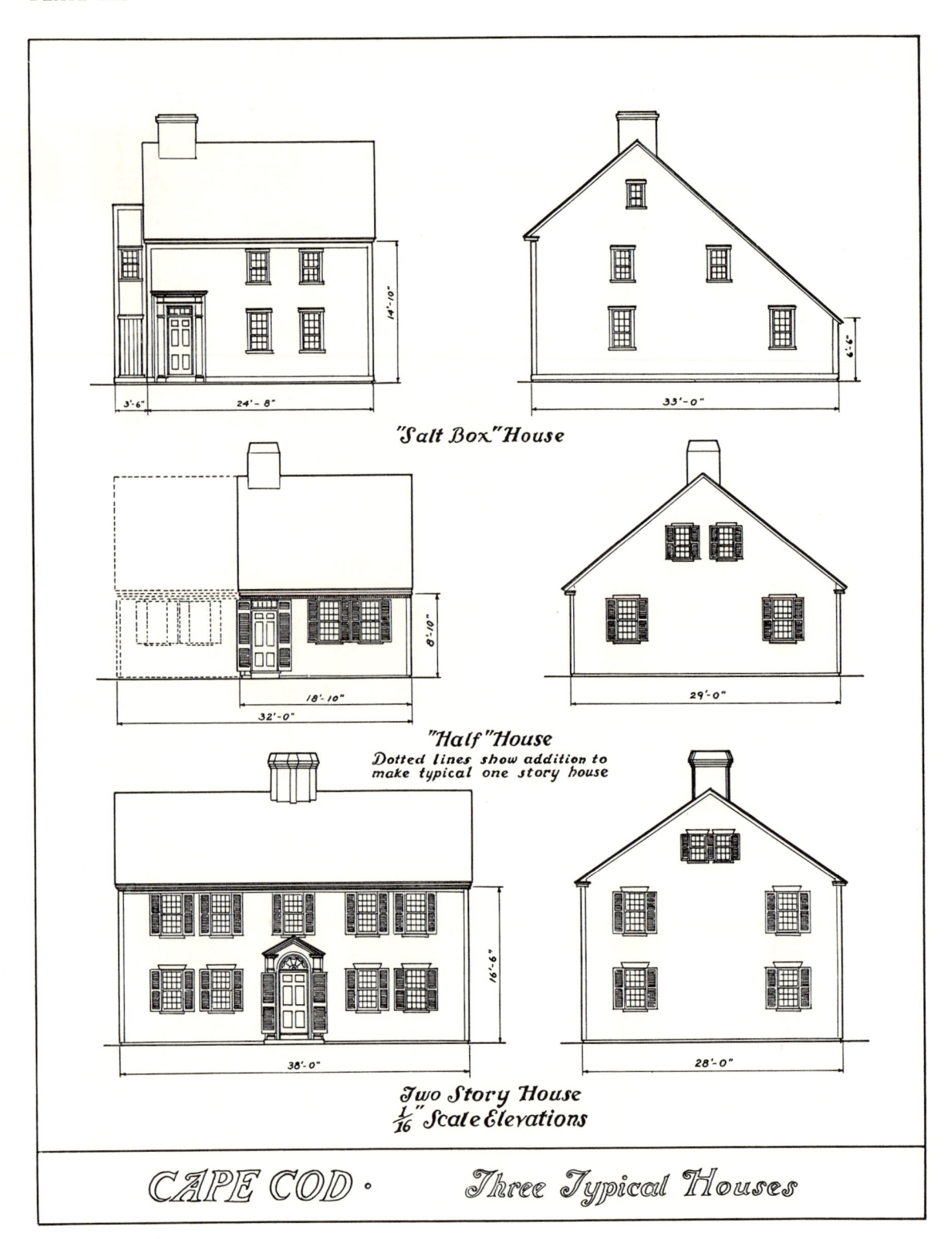

PLATE 118

"Salt Box" House

"Half" House
Dotted lines show addition to
make typical one story house

Two Story House
$\frac{1}{16}$" Scale Elevations

CAPE COD · Three Typical Houses

PLATE 119

½ Full Size Details   ½" Scale Elevation   3" Scale Detail

MOTOR CAR INN · DENNIS · Front Entrance

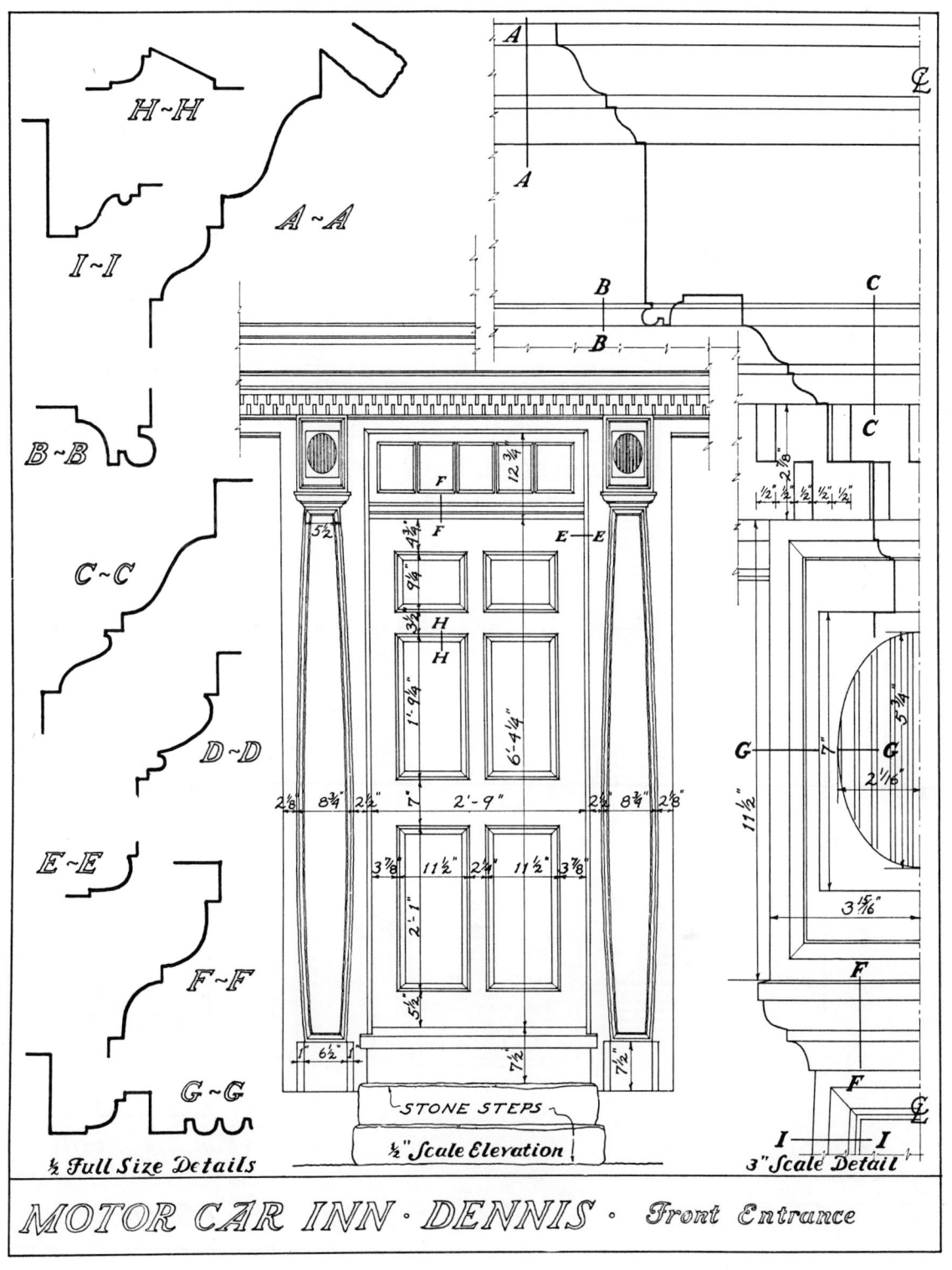

Illustration on Plate 73

PLATE 120

½ Full Size Details   ½" Scale Elevation   ½ Full Size Details

JUDGE FREAMAN HOUSE · DENNIS · Front Door

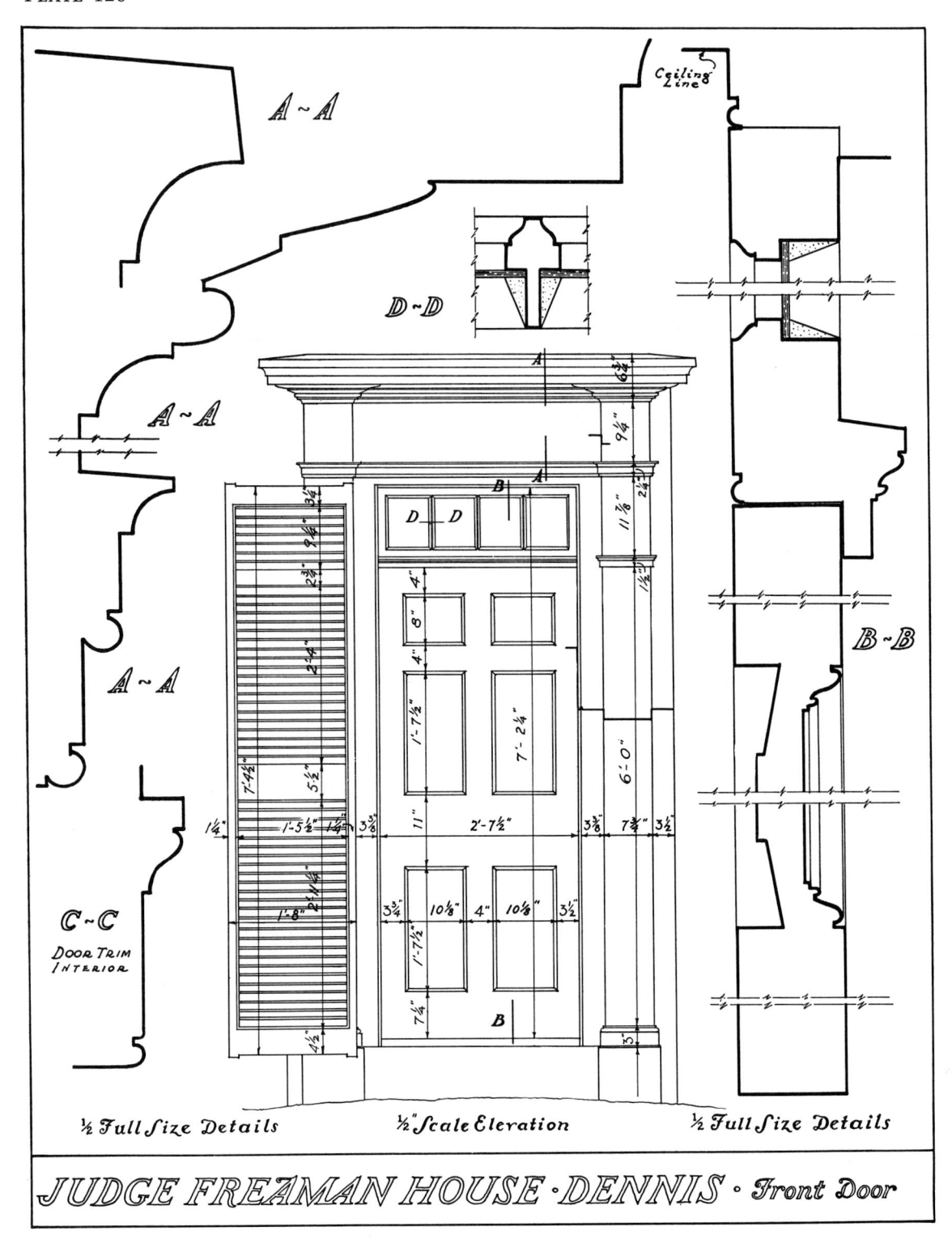

Illustration on Plate 73

PLATE 121

PROVINCETOWN — Typical Doorway

½ Full Size Details — C~C, D~D

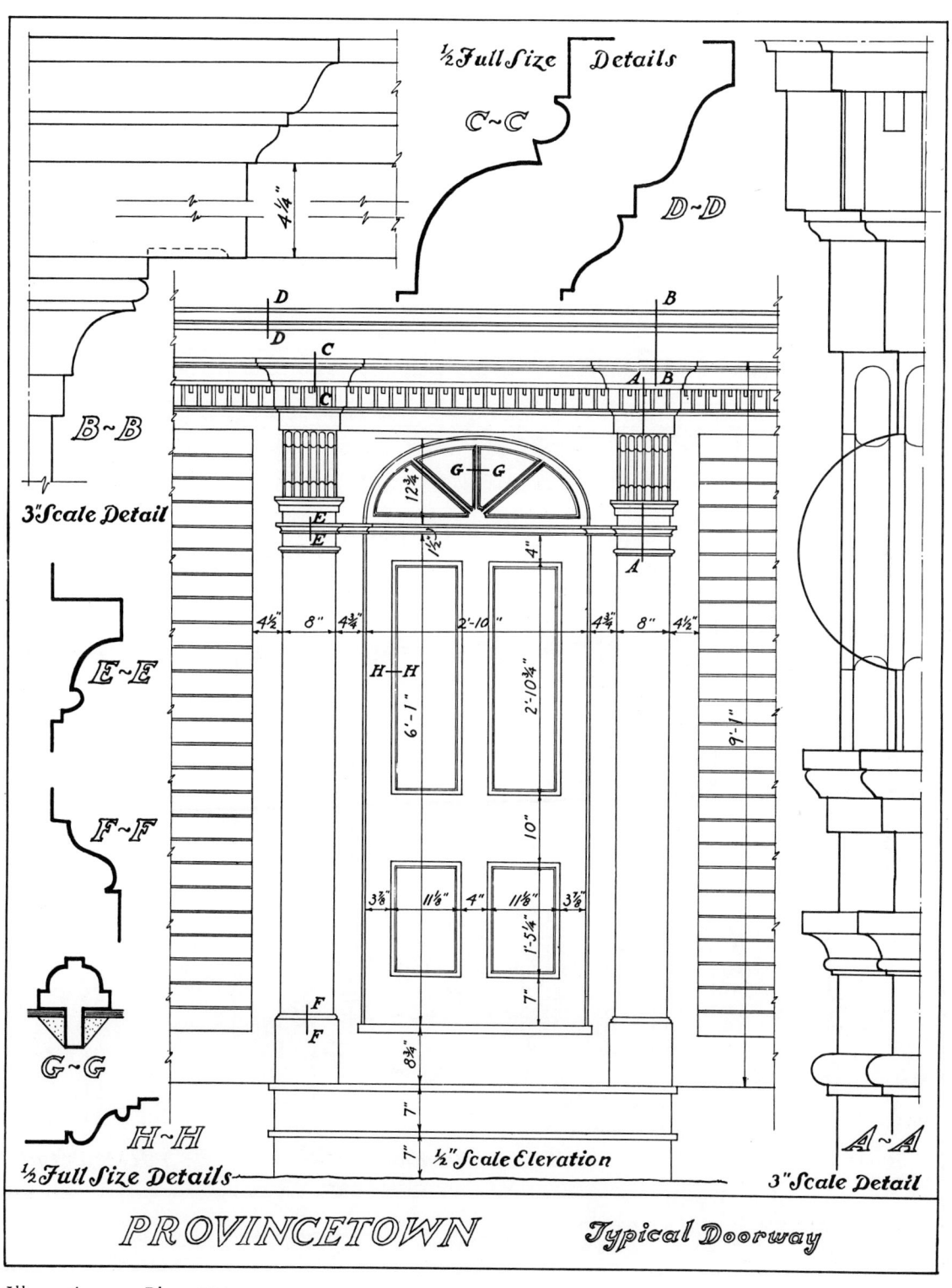

B~B — 3" Scale Detail

E~E, F~F, G~G, H~H — ½ Full Size Details

½" Scale Elevation

A~A — 3" Scale Detail

Illustration on Plate 78

PLATE 122

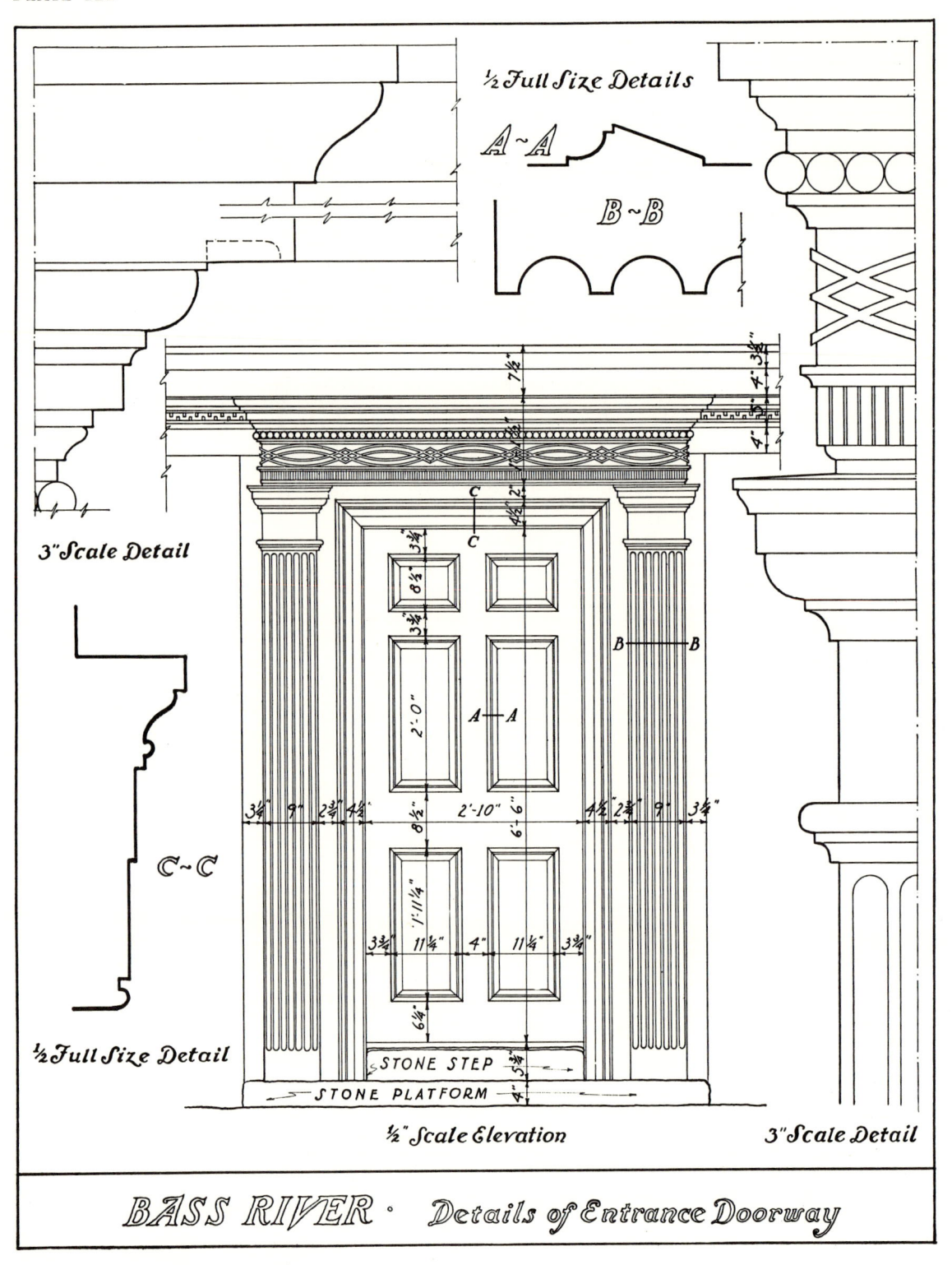

½ Full Size Details
A~A
B~B

3" Scale Detail

C~C

½ Full Size Detail

½" Scale Elevation

3" Scale Detail

BASS RIVER · Details of Entrance Doorway

Illustrations on Plates 15 and 74

PLATE 123

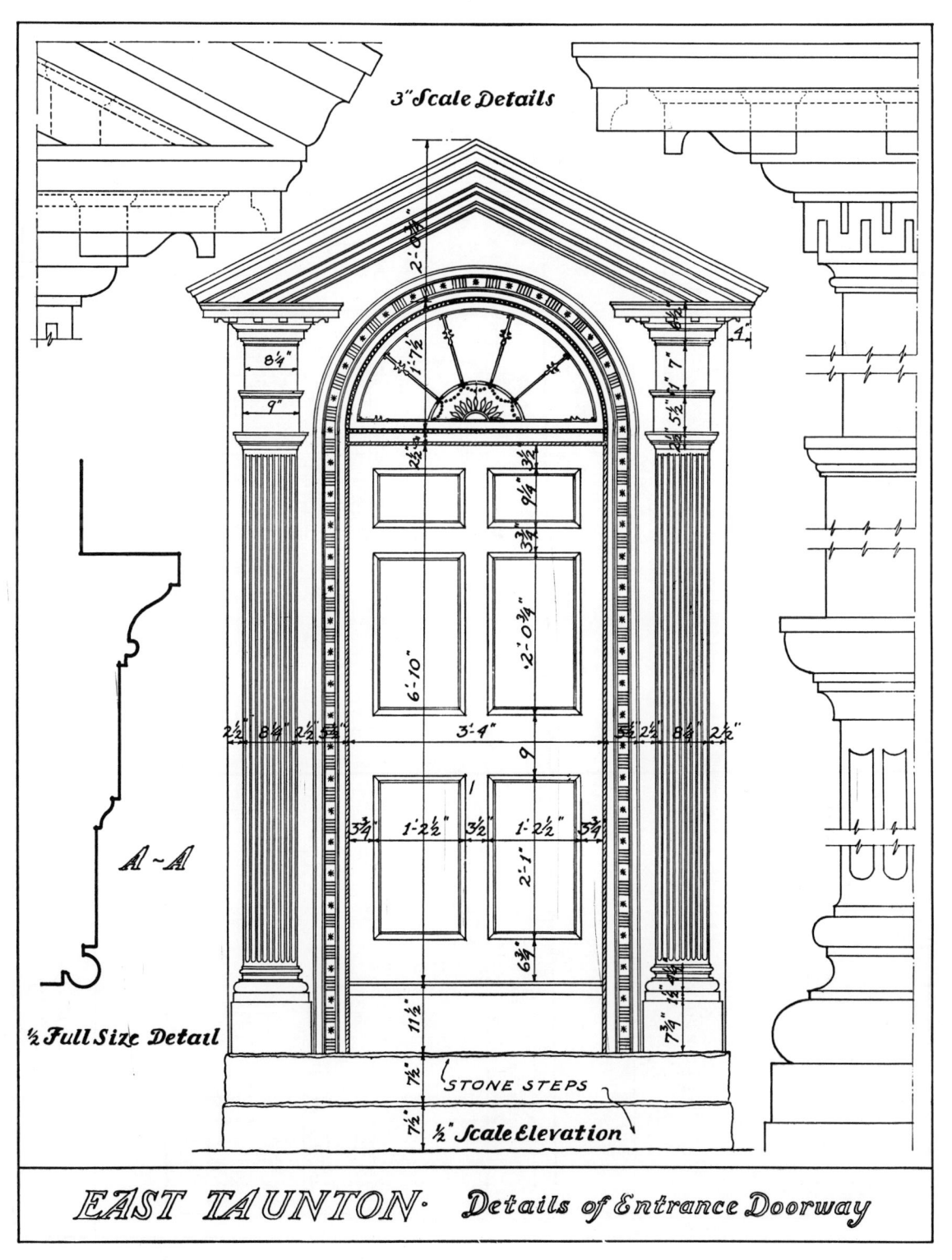

EAST TAUNTON · Details of Entrance Doorway

Illustration on Plate 80

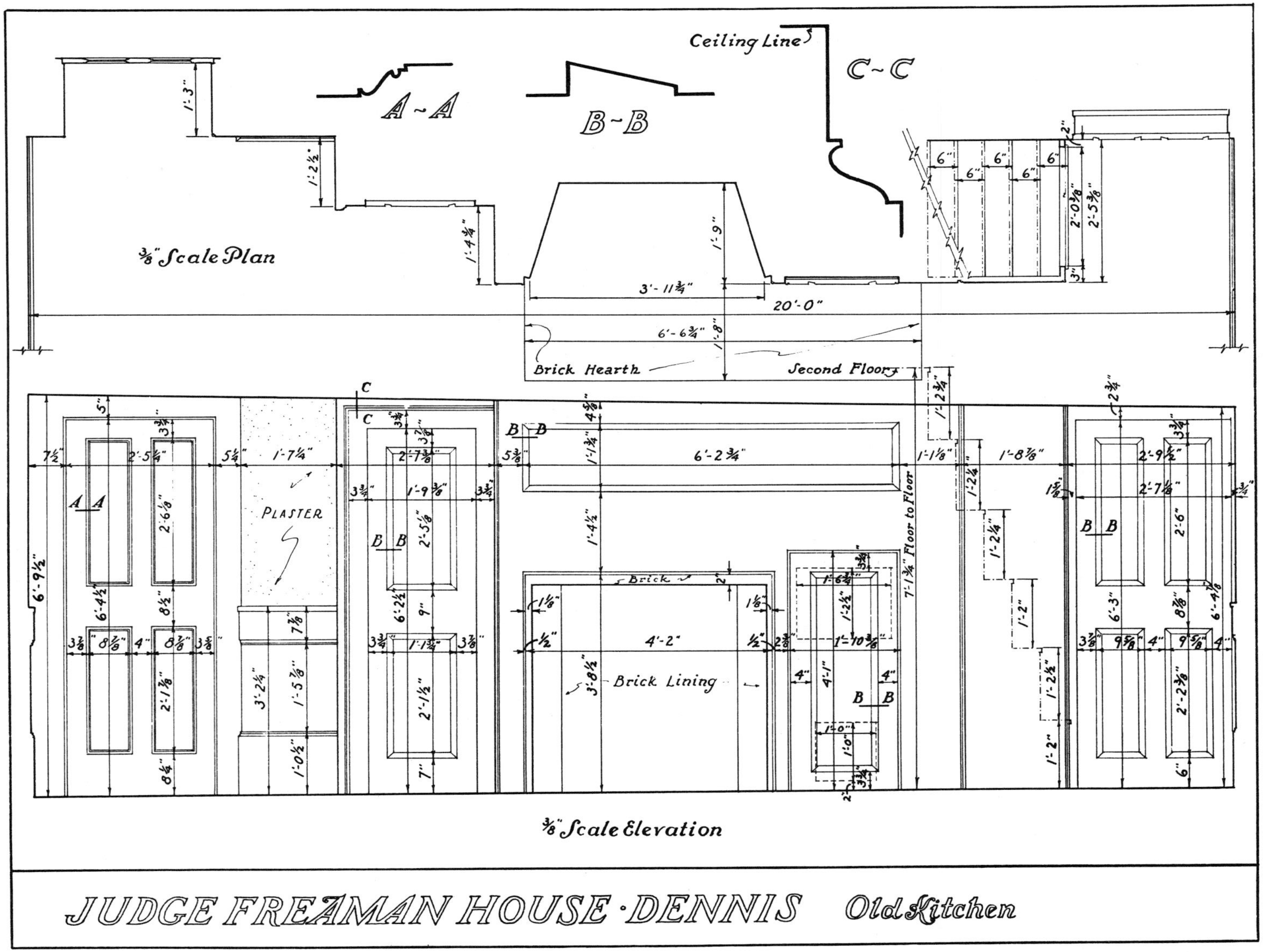

PLATE 124

JUDGE FREAMAN HOUSE · DENNIS   Old Kitchen

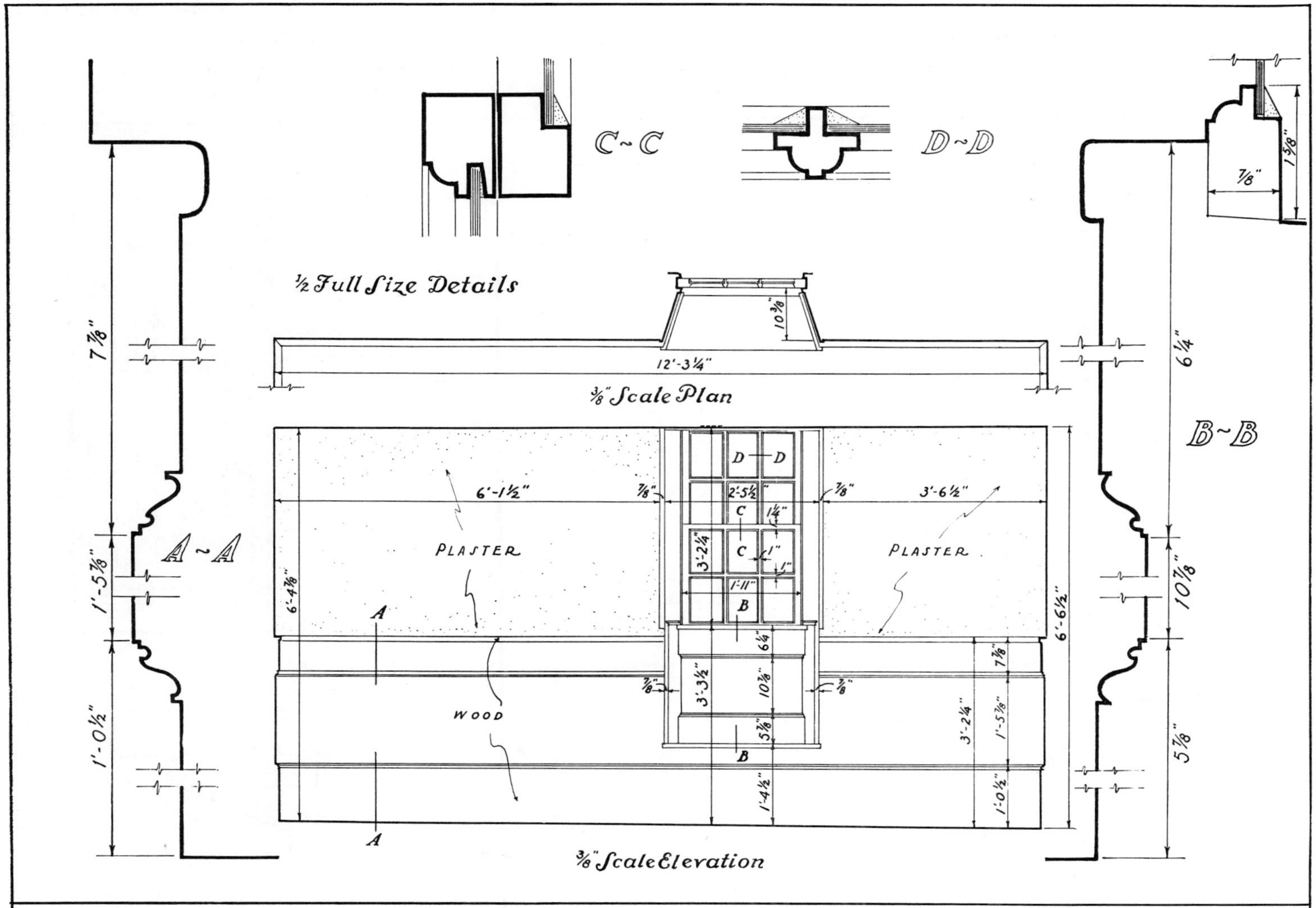

JUDGE FREAMAN HOUSE · DENNIS · *Old Kitchen*

½ Full Size Details

⅜" Scale Plan

⅜" Scale Elevation

Illustration on Plate 115

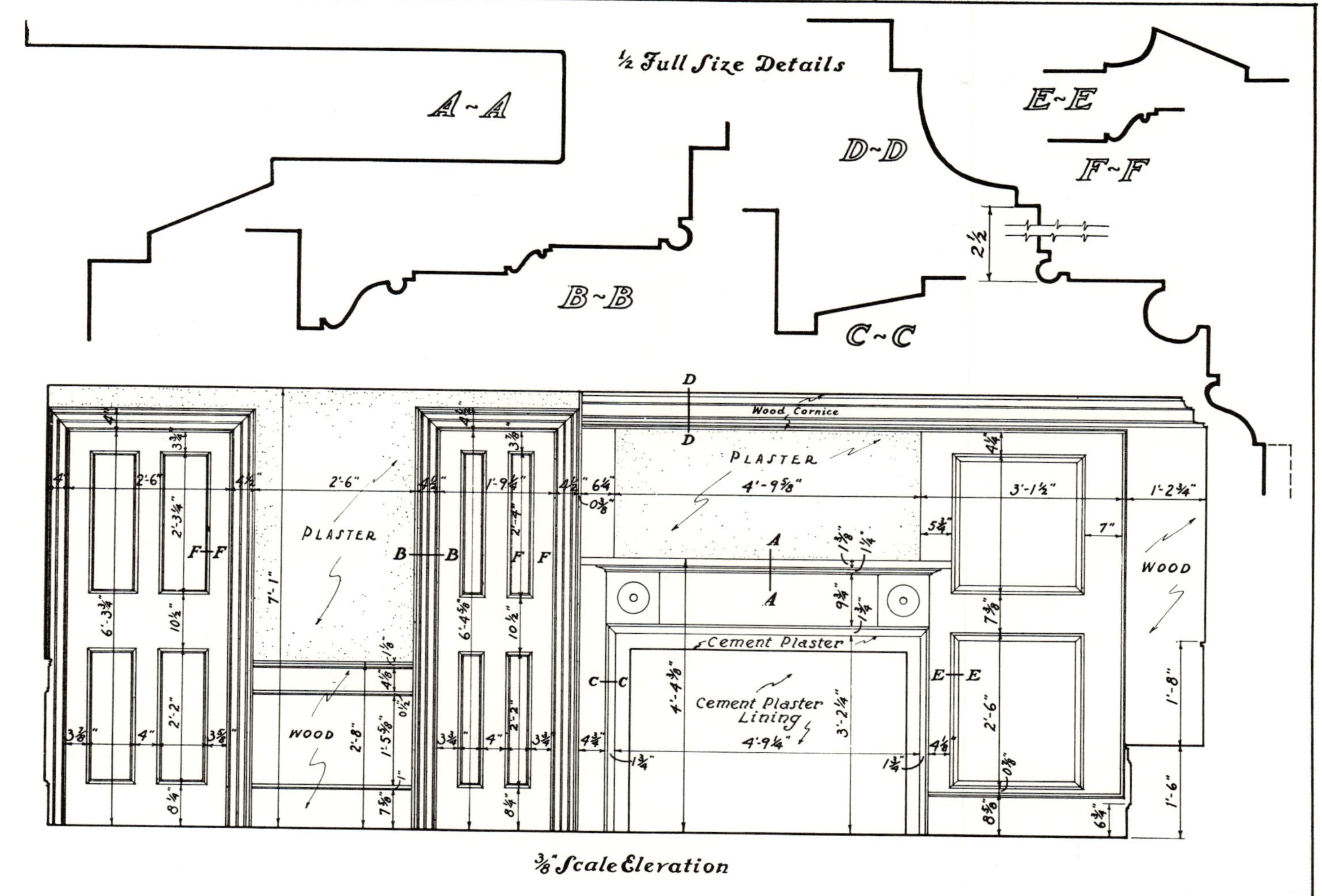

PLATE 126

½ Full Size Details

A~A
B~B
C~C
D~D
E~E
F~F

⅜" Scale Elevation

JUDGE FREAMAN HOUSE · DENNIS · Parlor

Illustration on Plate 117

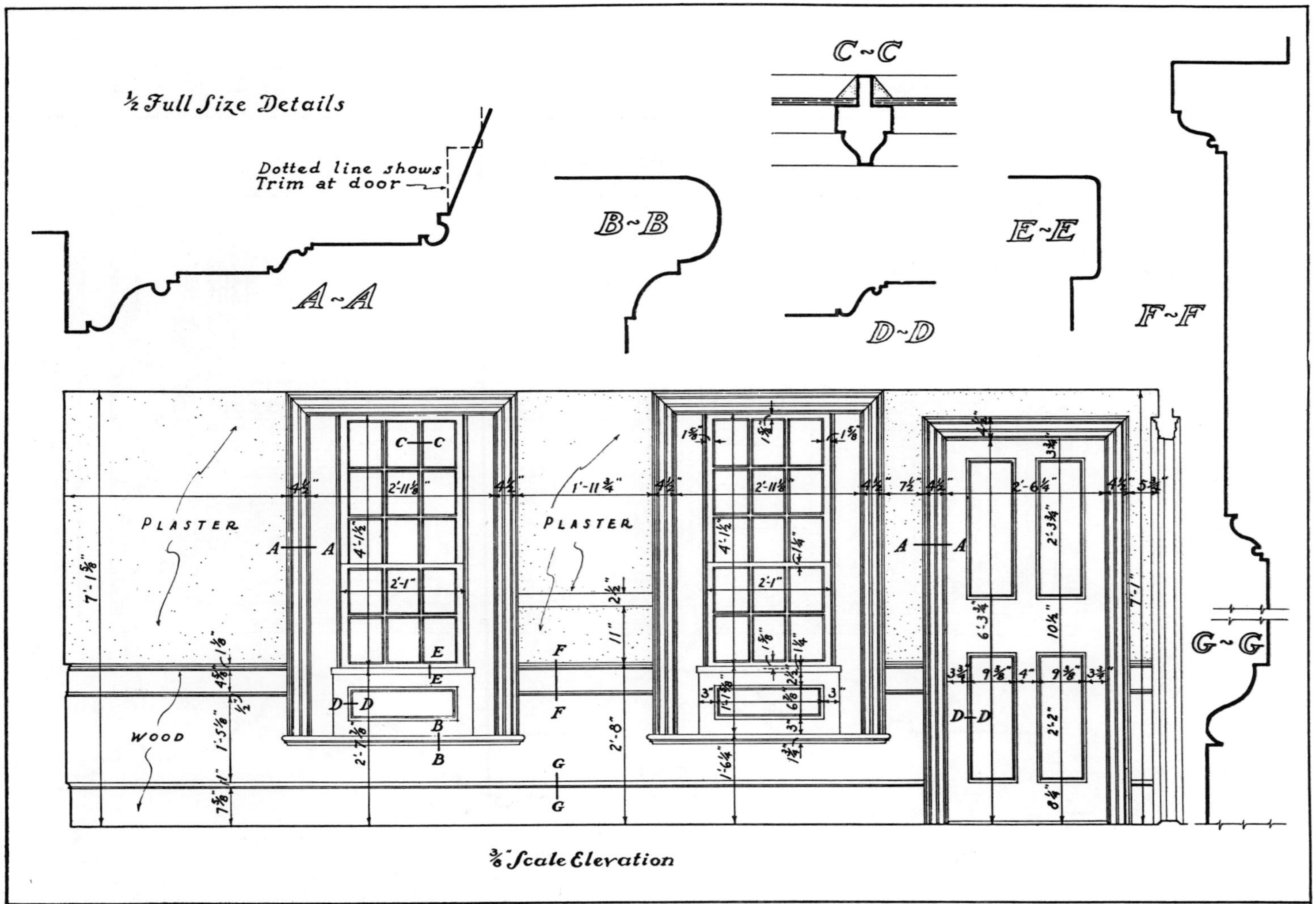

PLATE 127

½ Full Size Details

JUDGE FREAMAN HOUSE · DENNIS · *Parlor*

⅜" Scale Elevation

Illustration on Plate 115

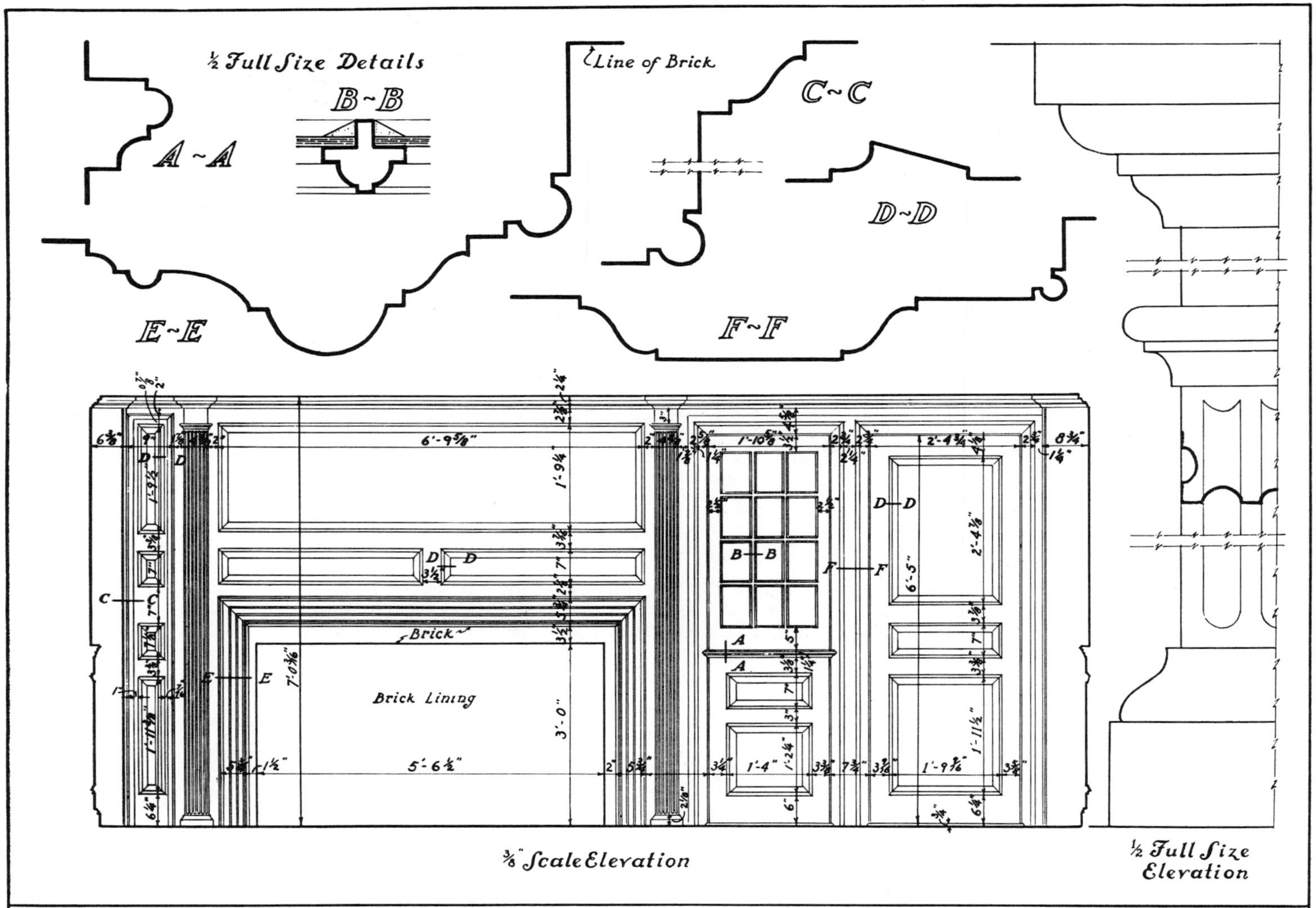

PLATE 128

JORGENSON HOUSE DENNIS. *Parlor*

½ Full Size Details
½ Full Size Elevation
⅜" Scale Elevation

Illustration on Plate 107

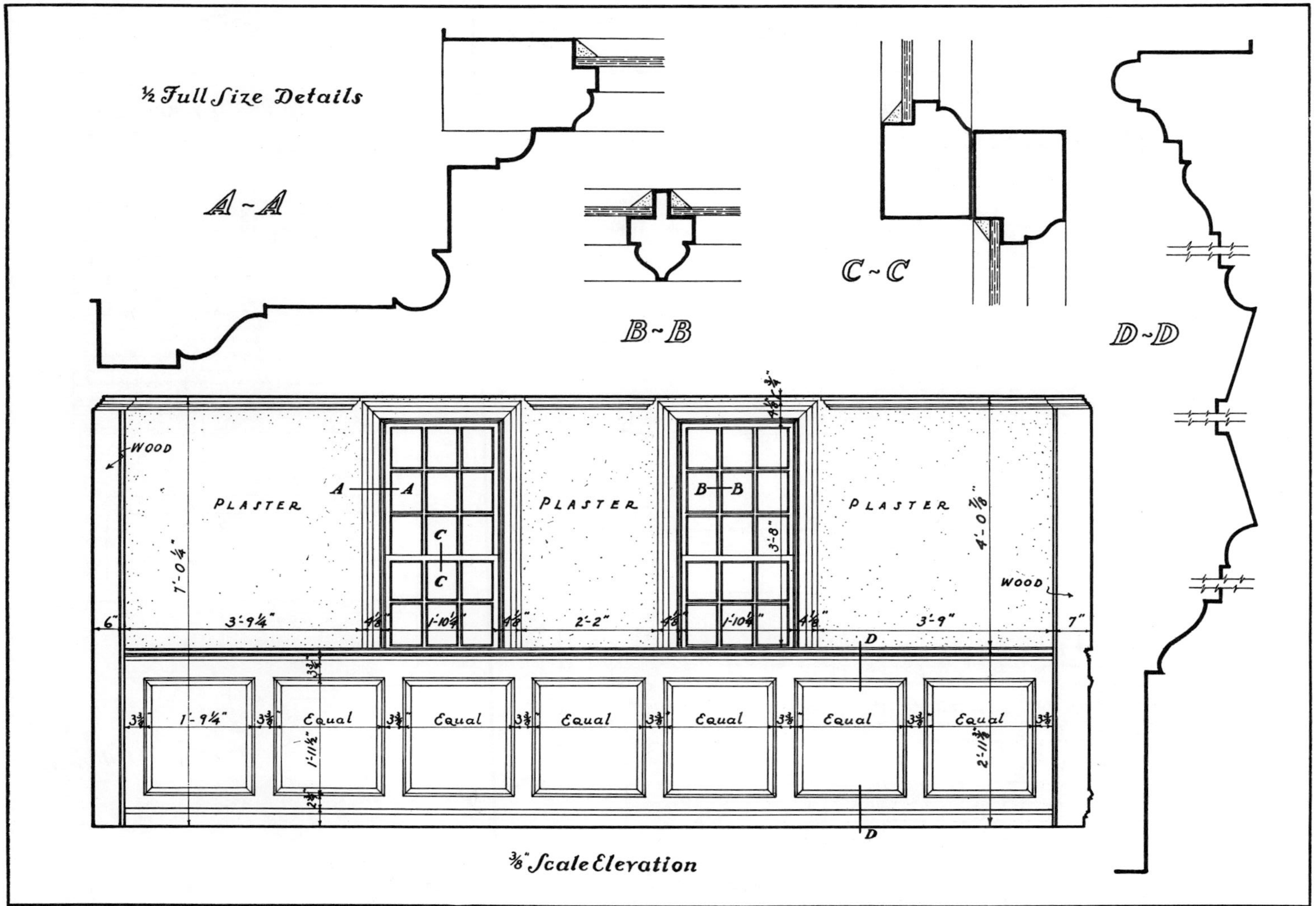

PLATE 129

½ Full Size Details

A~A

B~B

C~C

D~D

⅜" Scale Elevation

JORGENSON HOUSE · DENNIS · Parlor

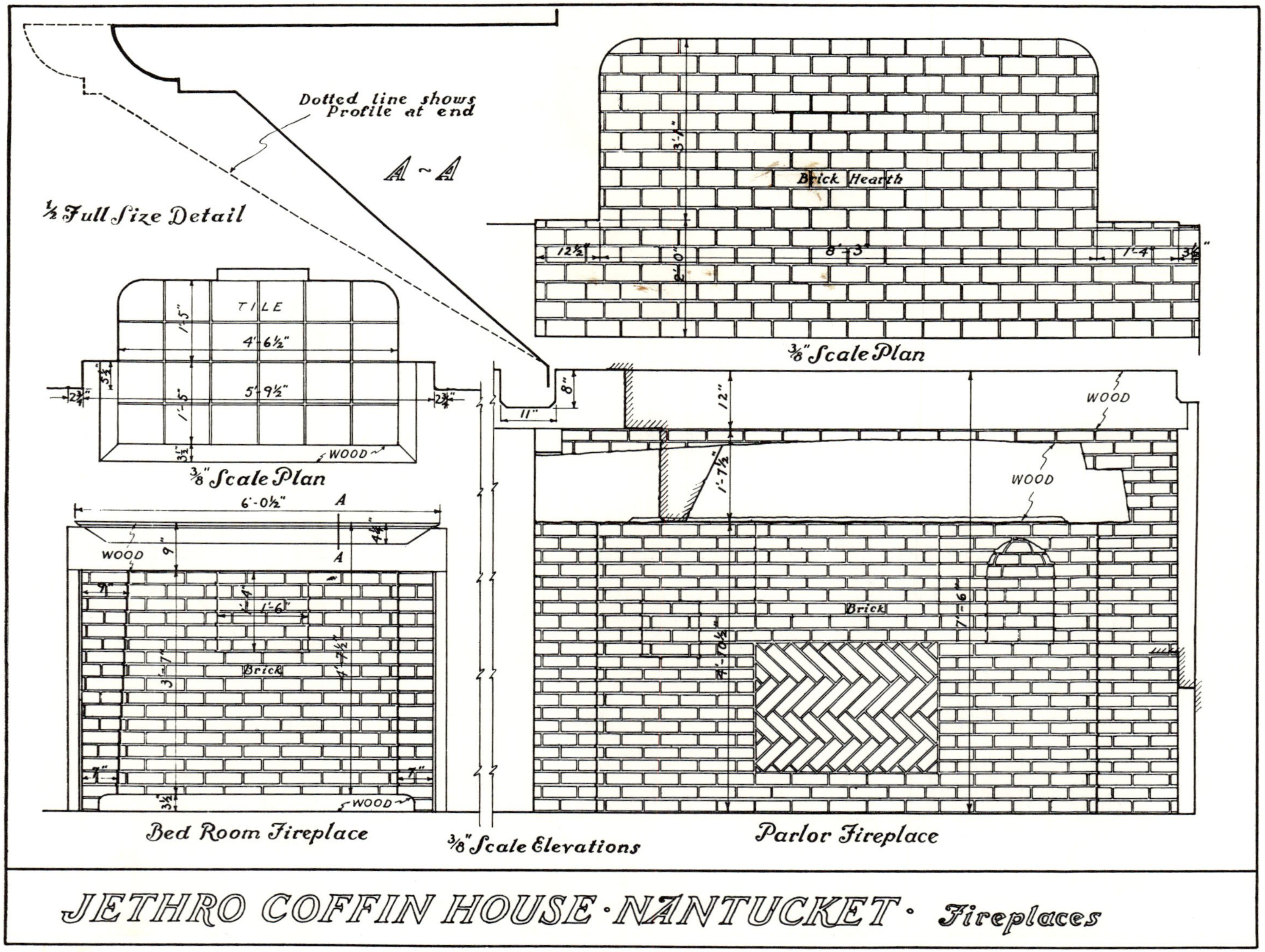

PLATE 130

JETHRO COFFIN HOUSE · NANTUCKET · Fireplaces

Illustration on Plate 102

PLATE 131

MOTOR CAR INN · DENNIS · Kitchen Fireplace

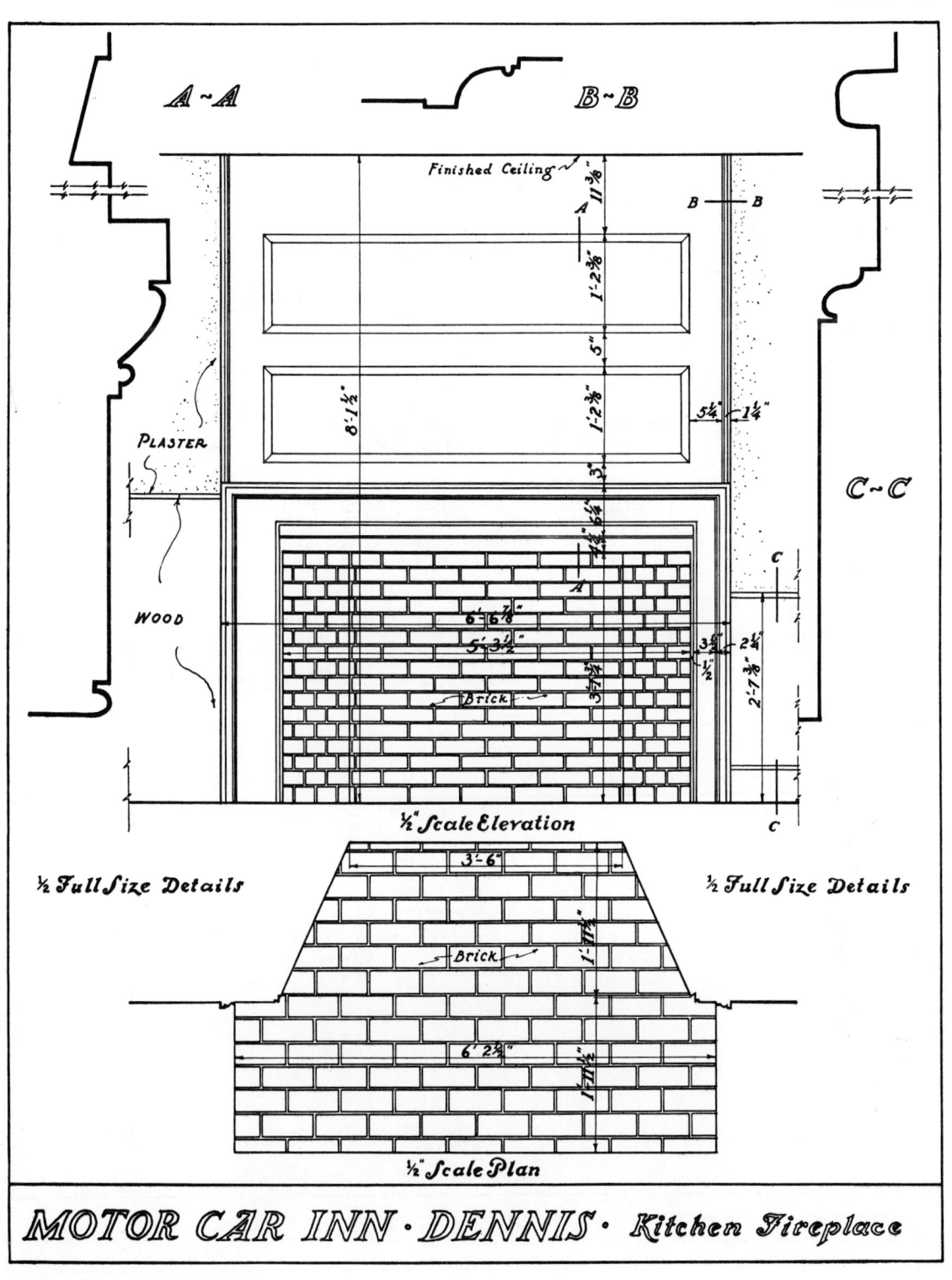

Illustration on Plate 109

PLATE 132

½ Full Size Details

A~A

B~B

Door Trim

½" Scale Elevation

Brick

Iron Band

½" Scale Plan

MOTOR CAR INN · DENNIS · Parlor Fireplace

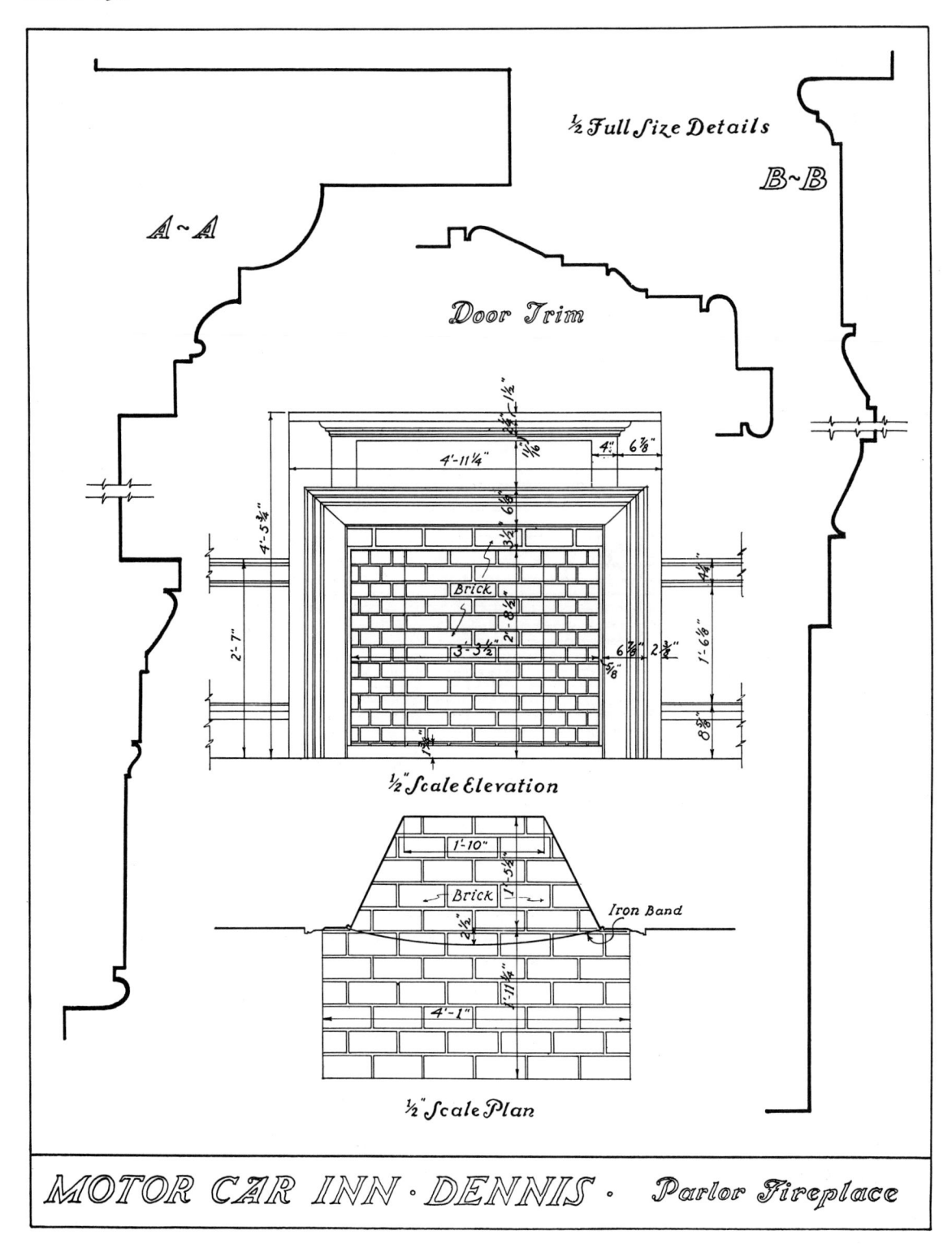

Illustration on Plate 110

PLATE 133

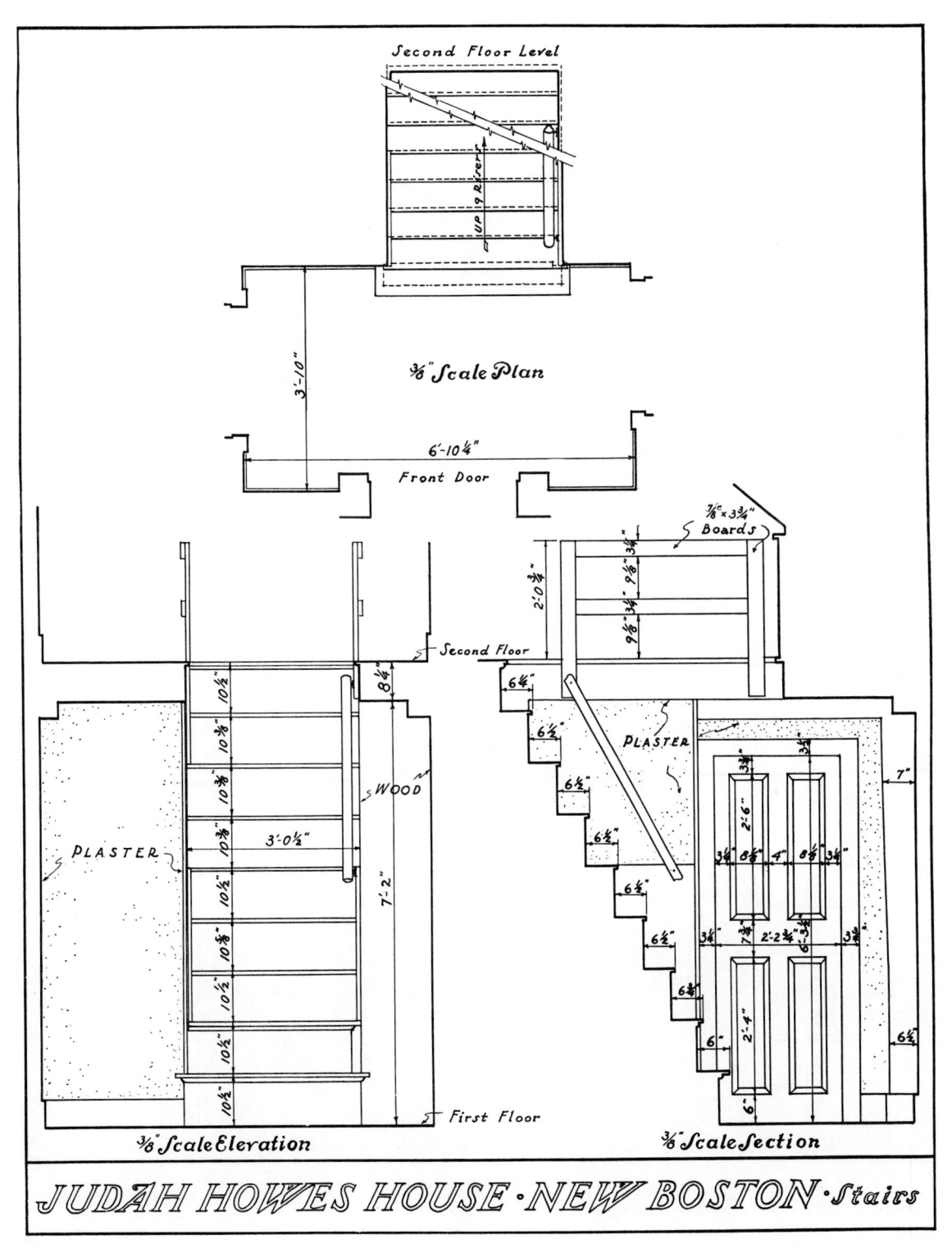

JUDAH HOWES HOUSE · NEW BOSTON · Stairs

Illustration on Plate 113

PLATE 134

JUDGE FREAMAN HOUSE · DENNIS · Stairway

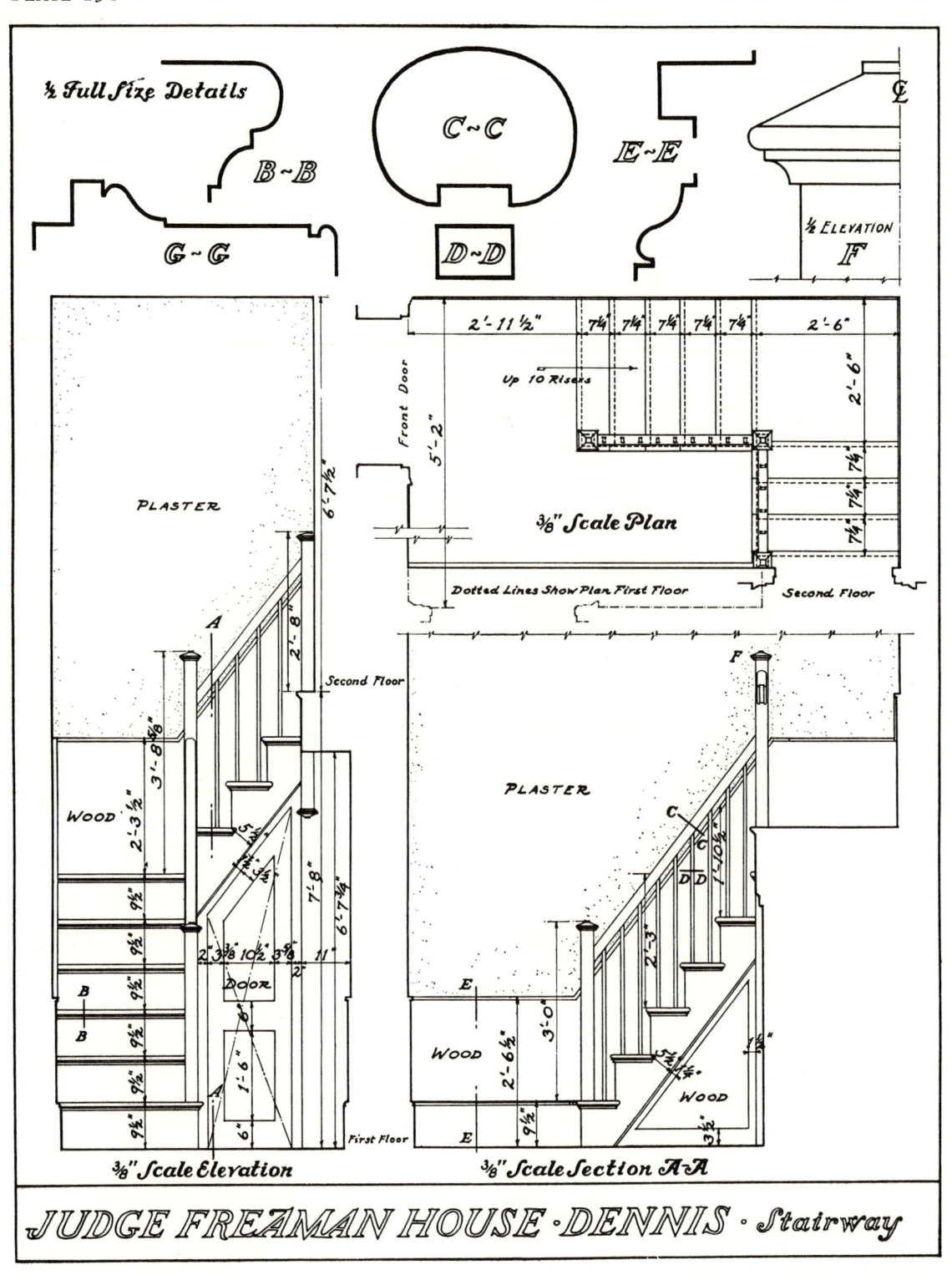

Illustration on Plate 113

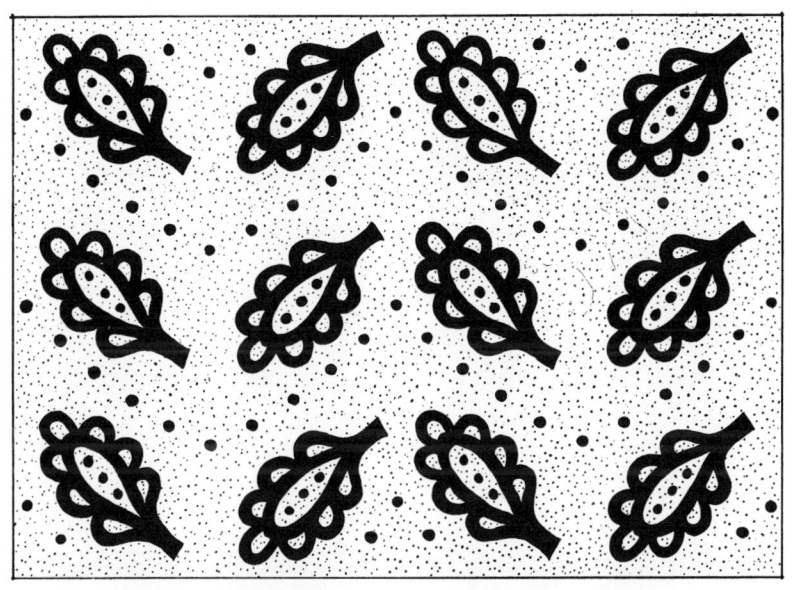

PLATE 135

Leaf Pattern from Barnstable
GROUND–BROWN; SPLATTER–DARK BROWN; DESIGN–BLACK

Typical Splatter Floor
1. GROUND–BLACK; SPLATTER–WHITE
2. GROUND–GREY; SPLATTER–WHITE
3. GROUND–BLUE; SPLATTER–WHITE
4. GROUND–GREEN; SPLATTER–WHITE
5. GROUND–VIOLET; SPLATTER–WHITE
6. GROUND–YELLOW; SPLATTER–BROWN

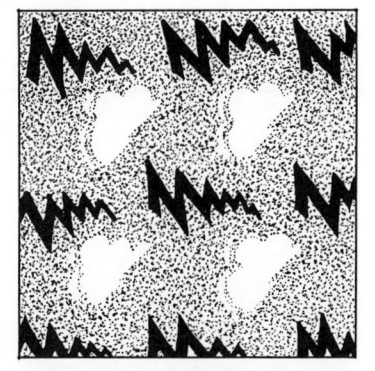

"Thunder and Lightning" from Old Tavern at Dennis
THUNDER – WHITE
LIGHTNING – BLUE
SPLATTER – BLUE
GROUND – GREY

½" Scale Details

CAPE COD — Typical Floor Patterns and Splatters

Dover Books on Art

Dover Books on Art

MASTERPIECES OF FURNITURE, Verna Cook Salomonsky. Photographs and measured drawings of some of the finest examples of Colonial American, 17th century English, Windsor, Sheraton, Hepplewhite, Chippendale, Louis XIV, Queen Anne, and various other furniture styles. The textual matter includes information on traditions, characteristics, background, etc. of various pieces. 101 plates. Bibliography. 224pp. 7⅞ x 10¾.
21381-1 Paperbound $3.00

PRIMITIVE ART, Franz Boas. In this exhaustive volume, a great American anthropologist analyzes all the fundamental traits of primitive art, covering the formal element in art, representative art, symbolism, style, literature, music, and the dance. Illustrations of Indian embroidery, paleolithic paintings, woven blankets, wing and tail designs, totem poles, cutlery, earthenware, baskets and many other primitive objects and motifs. Over 900 illustrations. 376pp. 5⅜ x 8.   20025-6 Paperbound $2.50

AN INTRODUCTION TO A HISTORY OF WOODCUT, A. M. Hind. Nearly all of this authoritative 2-volume set is devoted to the 15th century—the period during which the woodcut came of age as an important art form. It is the most complete compendium of information on this period, the artists who contributed to it, and their technical and artistic accomplishments. Profusely illustrated with cuts by 15th century masters, and later works for comparative purposes. 484 illustrations. 5 indexes. Total of xi + 838pp. 5⅜ x 8½. Two-vols. 20952-0, 20953-0 Paperbound $7.50

A HISTORY OF ENGRAVING AND ETCHING, A. M. Hind. Beginning with the anonymous masters of 15th century engraving, this highly regarded and thorough survey carries you through Italy, Holland, and Germany to the great engravers and beginnings of etching in the 16th century, through the portrait engravers, master etchers, practicioners of mezzotint, crayon manner and stipple, aquatint, color prints, to modern etching in the period just prior to World War I. Beautifully illustrated—sharp clear prints on heavy opaque paper. Author's preface. 3 appendixes. 111 illustrations. xviii + 487 pp. 5⅜ x 8½.
20954-7 Paperbound $3.50

ART STUDENTS' ANATOMY, E. J. Farris. Teaching anatomy by using chiefly living objects for illustration, this study has enjoyed long popularity and success in art courses and home-study programs. All the basic elements of the human anatomy are illustrated in minute detail, diagrammed and pictured as they pass through common movements and actions. 158 drawings, photographs, and roentgenograms. Glossary of anatomical terms. x + 159pp. 5⅝ x 8⅜.   20744-7 Paperbound $1.50

COLONIAL LIGHTING, A. H. Hayward. The only book to cover the fascinating story of lamps and other lighting devices in America. Beginning with rush light holders used by the early settlers, it ranges through the elaborate chandeliers of the Federal period, illustrating 647 lamps. Of great value to antique collectors, designers, and historians of arts and crafts. Revised and enlarged by James R. Marsh. xxxi + 198pp. 5⅝ x 8¼.
20975-X Paperbound $2.50

Dover Books on Art

PRINCIPLES OF ART HISTORY, H. Wölfflin. This remarkably instructive work demonstrates the tremendous change in artistic conception from the 14th to the 18th centuries, by analyzing 164 works by Botticelli, Dürer, Hobbema, Holbein, Hals, Titian, Rembrandt, Vermeer, etc., and pointing out exactly what is meant by "baroque," "classic," "primitive," "picturesque," and other basic terms of art history and criticism. "A remarkable lesson in the art of seeing," SAT. REV. OF LITERATURE. Translated from the 7th German edition. 150 illus. 254pp. 6⅛ x 9¼. 20276-3 Paperbound $2.50

FOUNDATIONS OF MODERN ART, A. Ozenfant. Stimulating discussion of human creativity from paleolithic cave painting to modern painting, architecture, decorative arts. Fully illustrated with works of Gris, Lipchitz, Léger, Picasso, primitive, modern artifacts, architecture, industrial art, much more. 226 illustrations. 368pp. 6⅛ x 9¼. 20215-1 Paperbound $3.00

METALWORK AND ENAMELLING, H. Maryon. Probably the best book ever written on the subject. Tells everything necessary for the home manufacture of jewelry, rings, ear pendants, bowls, etc. Covers materials, tools, soldering, filigree, setting stones, raising patterns, repoussé work, damascening, niello, cloisonné, polishing, assaying, casting, and dozens of other techniques. The best substitute for apprenticeship to a master metalworker. 363 photos and figures. 374pp. 5½ x 8½.
22702-2 Paperbound $3.50

SHAKER FURNITURE, E. D. and F. Andrews. The most illuminating study of Shaker furniture ever written. Covers chronology, craftsmanship, houses, shops, etc. Includes over 200 photographs of chairs, tables, clocks, beds, benches, etc. "Mr. & Mrs. Andrews know all there is to know about Shaker furniture," Mark Van Doren, NATION. 48 full-page plates. 192pp. 7⅞ x 10¾. 20679-3 Paperbound $2.75

LETTERING AND ALPHABETS, J. A. Cavanagh. An unabridged reissue of "Lettering," containing the full discussion, analysis, illustration of 89 basic hand lettering styles based on Caslon, Bodoni, Gothic, many other types. Hundreds of technical hints on construction, strokes, pens, brushes, etc. 89 alphabets, 72 lettered specimens, which may be reproduced permission-free. 121pp. 9¾ x 8. 20053-1 Paperbound $1.50

THE HUMAN FIGURE IN MOTION, Eadweard Muybridge. The largest collection in print of Muybridge's famous high-speed action photos. 4789 photographs in more than 500 action-strip-sequences (at shutter speeds up to 1/6000th of a second) illustrate men, women, children—mostly undraped—performing such actions as walking, running, getting up, lying down, carrying objects, throwing, etc. "An unparalleled dictionary of action for all artists," AMERICAN ARTIST. 390 full-page plates, with 4789 photographs. Heavy glossy stock, reinforced binding with headbands. 7⅞ x 10¾. 20204-6 Clothbound $12.50

Dover Books on Art

200 DECORATIVE TITLE-PAGES, edited by A. Nesbitt. Fascinating and informative from a historical point of view, this beautiful collection of decorated titles will be a great inspiration to students of design, commercial artists, advertising designers, etc. A complete survey of the genre from the first known decorated title to work in the first decades of this century. Bibliography and sources of the plates. 222pp. 8⅜ x 11¼.
21264-5 Paperbound $3.50

ON THE LAWS OF JAPANESE PAINTING, H. P. Bowie. This classic work on the philosophy and technique of Japanese art is based on the author's first-hand experiences studying art in Japan. Every aspect of Japanese painting is described: the use of the brush and other materials; laws governing conception and execution; subjects for Japanese paintings, etc. The best possible substitute for a series of lessons from a great Oriental master. Index. xv + 117pp. + 66 plates. 6⅛ x 9¼.
20030-2 Paperbound $2.50

A HANDBOOK OF ANATOMY FOR ART STUDENTS, Arthur Thomson. This long-popular text teaches any student, regardless of level of technical competence, all the subtleties of human anatomy. Clear photographs, numerous line sketches and diagrams of bones, joints, etc. Use it as a text for home study, as a supplement to life class work, or as a lifelong sourcebook and reference volume. Author's prefaces. 67 plates, containing 40 line drawings, 86 photographs—mostly full page. 211 figures. Appendix. Index. xx + 459pp. 5⅜ x 8⅜. 21163-0 Paperbound $3.50

WHITTLING AND WOODCARVING, E. J. Tangerman. With this book, a beginner who is moderately handy can whittle or carve scores of useful objects, toys for children, gifts, or simply pass hours creatively and enjoyably. "Easy as well as instructive reading," N. Y. Herald Tribune Books. 464 illustrations, with appendix and index. x + 293pp. 5½ x 8⅛.
20965-2 Paperbound $2.00

ONE HUNDRED AND ONE PATCHWORK PATTERNS, Ruby Short McKim. Whether you have made a hundred quilts or none at all, you will find this the single most useful book on quiltmaking. There are 101 full patterns (all exact size) with full instructions for cutting and sewing. In addition there is some really choice folklore about the origin of the ingenious pattern names: "Monkey Wrench," "Road to California," "Drunkard's Path," "Crossed Canoes," to name a few. Over 500 illustrations. 124 pp. 7⅞ x 10¾. 20773-0 Paperbound $2.00

ART AND GEOMETRY, W. M. Ivins, Jr. Challenges the idea that the foundations of modern thought were laid in ancient Greece. Pitting Greek tactile-muscular intuitions of space against modern visual intuitions, the author, for 30 years curator of prints, Metropolitan Museum of Art, analyzes the differences between ancient and Renaissance painting and sculpture and tells of the first fruitful investigations of perspective. x + 113pp. 5⅜ x 8⅜. 20941-5 Paperbound $1.50

Dover Books on Art

ART ANATOMY, Dr. William Rimmer. One of the few books on art anatomy that are themselves works of art, this is a faithful reproduction (rearranged for handy use) of the extremely rare masterpiece of the famous 19th century anatomist, sculptor, and art teacher. Beautiful, clear line drawings show every part of the body—bony structure, muscles, features, etc. Unusual are the sections on falling bodies, foreshortenings, muscles in tension, grotesque personalities, and Rimmer's remarkable interpretation of emotions and personalities as expressed by facial features. It will supplement every other book on art anatomy you are likely to have. Reproduced clearer than the lithographic original (which sells for $500 on up on the rare book market.) Over 1,200 illustrations. xiii + 153pp. 7¾ x 10¾.
20908-3 Paperbound $2.50

THE CRAFTSMAN'S HANDBOOK, Cennino Cennini. The finest English translation of IL LIBRO DELL' ARTE, the 15th century introduction to art technique that is both a mirror of Quatrocento life and a source of many useful but nearly forgotten facets of the painter's art. 4 illustrations. xxvii + 142pp. D. V. Thompson, translator. 5⅜ x 8.
20054-X Paperbound $2.00

THE BROWN DECADES, Lewis Mumford. A picture of the "buried renaissance" of the post-Civil War period, and the founding of modern architecture (Sullivan, Richardson, Root, Roebling), landscape development (Marsh, Olmstead, Eliot), and the graphic arts (Homer, Eakins, Ryder). 2nd revised, enlarged edition. Bibliography. 12 illustrations. xiv + 266 pp. 5⅜ x 8.
20200-3 Paperbound $2.00

THE STYLES OF ORNAMENT, A. Speltz. The largest collection of line ornament in print, with 3750 numbered illustrations arranged chronologically from Egypt, Assyria, Greeks, Romans, Etruscans, through Medieval, Renaissance, 18th century, and Victorian. No permissions, no fees needed to use or reproduce illustrations. 400 plates with 3750 illustrations. Bibliography. Index. 640pp. 6 x 9.
20577-6 Paperbound $3.75

THE ART OF ETCHING, E. S. Lumsden. Every step of the etching process from essential materials to completed proof is carefully and clearly explained, with 24 annotated plates exemplifying every technique and approach discussed. The book also features a rich survey of the art, with 105 annotated plates by masters. Invaluable for beginner to advanced etcher. 374pp. 5⅜ x 8.
20049-3 Paperbound $3.00

OF THE JUST SHAPING OF LETTERS, Albrecht Dürer. This remarkable volume reveals Albrecht Dürer's rules for the geometric construction of Roman capitals and the formation of Gothic lower case and capital letters, complete with construction diagrams and directions. Of considerable practical interest to the contemporary illustrator, artist, and designer. Translated from the Latin text of the edition of 1535 by R. T. Nichol. Numerous letterform designs, construction diagrams, illustrations. iv + 43pp. 7⅞ x 10¾.
21306-4 Paperbound $2.00

Dover Books on Art

GREEK REVIVAL ARCHITECTURE IN AMERICA, T. Hamlin. A comprehensive study of the American Classical Revival, its regional variations, reasons for its success and eventual decline. Profusely illustrated with photos, sketches, floor plans and sections, displaying the work of almost every important architect of the time. 2 appendices. 39 figures, 94 plates containing 221 photos, 62 architectural designs, drawings, etc. 324-item classified bibliography. Index. xi + 439pp. 5⅜ x 8½.

21148-7 Paperbound $4.50

CREATIVE LITHOGRAPHY AND HOW TO DO IT, Grant Arnold. Written by a man who practiced and taught lithography for many years, this highly useful volume explains all the steps of the lithographic process from tracing the drawings on the stone to printing the lithograph, with helpful hints for solving special problems. Index. 16 reproductions of lithographs. 11 drawings. xv + 214pp. of text. 5⅜ x 8½.

21208-4 Paperbound $3.00

TEACH YOURSELF ANTIQUE COLLECTING, E. Bradford. An excellent, brief guide to collecting British furniture, silver, pictures and prints, pewter, pottery and porcelain, Victoriana, enamels, clocks or other antiques. Much background information difficult to find elsewhere. 15pp. of illus. 215pp. 7 x 4¼.

21368-4 Clothbound $2.50

PAINTING IN THE FAR EAST, L. Binyon. A study of over 1500 years of Oriental art by one of the world's outstanding authorities. The author chooses the most important masters in each period—Wu Tao-tzu, Toba Sojo, Kanaoka, Li Lung-mien, Masanobu, Okio, etc.—and examines the works, schools, and influence of each within their cultural context. 42 photographs. Sources of original works and selected bibliography. Notes including list of principal painters by periods. xx + 297pp. 6⅛ x 9¼.

20520-7 Paperbound $5.00

THE ALPHABET AND ELEMENTS OF LETTERING, F. W. Goudy. A beautifully illustrated volume on the aesthetics of letters and type faces and their history and development. Each plate consists of 15 forms of a single letter with the last plate devoted to the ampersand and the numerals. "A sound guide for all persons engaged in printing or drawing," Saturday Review. 27 full-page plates. 48 additional figures. xii + 131pp. 7⅞ x 10¾.

20792-7 Paperbound $2.50

THE COMPLETE BOOK OF SILK SCREEN PRINTING PRODUCTION, J. I. Biegeleisen. Here is a clear and complete picture of every aspect of silk screen technique and press operation—from individually operated manual presses to modern automatic ones. Unsurpassed as a guidebook for setting up shop, making shop operation more efficient, finding out about latest methods and equipment; or as a textbook for use in teaching, studying, or learning all aspects of the profession. 124 figures. Index. Bibliography. List of Supply Sources. xi + 253pp. 5⅜ x 8½.

21100-2 Paperbound $2.75

Dover Books on Art

LANDSCAPE GARDENING IN JAPAN, Josiah Conder. A detailed picture of Japanese gardening techniques and ideas, the artistic principles incorporated in the Japanese garden, and the religious and ethical concepts at the heart of those principles. Preface. 92 illustrations, plus all 40 full-page plates from the Supplement. Index. xv + 299pp. 8⅜ x 11¼.
21216-5 Paperbound $4.50

DESIGN AND FIGURE CARVING, E. J. Tangerman. "Anyone who can peel a potato can carve," states the author, and in this unusual book he shows you how, covering every stage in detail from very simple exercises working up to museum-quality pieces. Terrific aid for hobbyists, arts and crafts counselors, teachers, those who wish to make reproductions for the commercial market. Appendix: How to Enlarge a Design. Brief bibliography. Index. 1298 figures. x + 289pp. 5⅜ x 8½.
21209-2 Paperbound $3.00

THE STANDARD BOOK OF QUILT MAKING AND COLLECTING, M. Ickis. Even if you are a beginner, you will soon find yourself quilting like an expert, by following these clearly drawn patterns, photographs, and step-by-step instructions. Learn how to plan the quilt, to select the pattern to harmonize with the design and color of the room, to choose materials. Over 40 full-size patterns. Index. 483 illustrations. One color plate. xi + 276pp. 6¾ x 9½.
20582-7 Paperbound $3.50

LOST EXAMPLES OF COLONIAL ARCHITECTURE, J. M. Howells. This book offers a unique guided tour through America's architectural past, all of which is either no longer in existence or so changed that its original beauty has been destroyed. More than 275 clear photos of old churches, dwelling houses, public buildings, business structures, etc. 245 plates, containing 281 photos and 9 drawings, floorplans, etc. New Index. xvii + 248pp. 7⅞ x 10¾.
21143-6 Paperbound $3.50

A HISTORY OF COSTUME, Carl Köhler. The most reliable and authentic account of the development of dress from ancient times through the 19th century. Based on actual pieces of clothing that have survived, using paintings, statues and other reproductions only where originals no longer exist. Hundreds of illustrations, including detailed patterns for many articles. Highly useful for theatre and movie directors, fashion designers, illustrators, teachers. Edited and augmented by Emma von Sichart. Translated by Alexander K. Dallas. 594 illustrations. 464pp. 5⅛ x 7⅞.
21030-8 Paperbound $3.50

Dover publishes books on commercial art, art history, crafts, design, art classics; also books on music, literature, science, mathematics, puzzles and entertainments, chess, engineering, biology, philosophy, psychology, languages, history, and other fields. For free circulars write to Dept. DA, Dover Publications, Inc., 180 Varick St., New York, N.Y. 10014.